A DYNASTY BEGINS

THE KANSAS CITY CHIEFS' 2022 CHAMPIONSHIP SEASON

*To my father, Pete Sr., who instilled in me a love of pro sports —
and the significance they hold in our lives.*

*And to my mother, Denise, who has provided unwavering support through
all my ups and downs, both career and otherwise.*

Without these individuals, this project never would have been possible.

—P.S.

This book is available in quantity at special discounts for your group or organization.
For further information, contact:

Triumph Books LLC
814 North Franklin Street
Chicago, Illinois 60610
Phone: (312) 337-0747
www.triumphbooks.com

Printed in U.S.A.
ISBN: 978-1- 63727-520-7

Content packaged by Mojo Media, Inc.
Joe Funk: Editor
Jason Hinman: Creative Director

Except where otherwise noted, all photos by AP Images

CONTENTS

FOREWORD

by Mitchell Schwartz

The road to the Kansas City Chiefs' Super Bowl LVII championship began on the night of February 7, 2021, as my team, the Chiefs, traveled down to Tampa Bay to take on the Buccaneers in Super Bowl LV.

As a team, we had a crystal-clear goal — get back to the Super Bowl and win it. Run it back and become the first team since the New England Patriots of the early 2000s to bring home back-to-back titles.

And though we came so close to pulling it off, a glaring weakness reared its head on the season's final night.

We needed to be deeper when it came to our offensive line. I was injured, Eric Fisher was injured, Kelechi Osemele was injured — and Laurent Duvernay-Tardif and Lucas Niang had opted out. Our line was depleted, and we were up against the best defensive front in the league.

Unprotected and pressured on more than half of his drop backs, Patrick Mahomes could only do so much, and we lost in a blowout, 31-9.

The reason I say the road to 2022's title began on that night is because it was a clear turning point for the organization. Not only did general manager Brett Veach and his staff want a stronger, healthier offensive line; they also wanted to fill the room with solid depth.

The next time the Chiefs played a football game, the offensive line room would be eight, nine, or 10 players deep. Veach wanted to find a way to ensure a night like that never happened for Mahomes again.

The Super Bowl LVII win over the Philadelphia Eagles was the Chiefs very literally reaping the decision of that night, as well as what followed: Andrew Wylie and Niang took over my spot. The Chiefs signed Joe Thuney, traded for Orlando Brown Jr., and drafted Creed Humphrey and Trey Smith. Nick Allegretti remained on the club as the ultimate utility man, with Prince Tega Wanogho, Austin Reiter, and Darian Kinnard rounding out the room.

The Chiefs made the tough decision to move on from Tyreek Hill, and like he has done so many times before (and for both of the franchises included in this year's Super Bowl), Andy Reid had to reinvent the offense, adjusting to weekly defensive structures designed to take away the explosive, down-field passing attack. The offense had to learn to play more down to down and lay into the run game when necessary — drive it down the field, step by step.

Meanwhile, the defense learned that leaning into rookies and first and second-year players will come with its mistakes, but it will be better for it in the long run. One of the more underrated parts of watching these Super Bowl-winning Chiefs was the growth of Steve Spagnuolo's youthful bunch from Week 1 to the night they lifted the Lombardi.

Mahomes put together his second MVP season, Travis Kelce, now without Hill, found ways to continue to get open — and open in the end zone. Chris Jones was a finalist for Defensive Player of the Year.

The Chiefs did not allow one bad half against a Cincinnati Bengals team to ruin their long-term plan, which was to persist in its infusion of young talent and grow together.

Quarterback Patrick Mahomes celebrates the Chiefs' victory following Super Bowl LVII at State Farm Stadium in Glendale.

As I took in this year of football for the first time as a retired player, that is what sticks out to me about the 2022 Chiefs — *growing together,* in and around Mahomes, who has fully separated himself as the game's best quarterback at the age of 27.

Mahomes' resume has been unmatched through his first five years as a starter in the course of NFL history. It includes nearly 24,000 yards, nearly 200 touchdowns, and MVPs for the 2018 and 2022 seasons.

What has always impressed me the most about Mahomes — and continues to impress me to this day — are the parts most don't get to see. He is unsatisfied through his half-decade of dominance; his competitiveness drives him never to stop improving.

In 2022, he took his game a further step in showing how it is not defined by one pass-catcher, and like many of the greats, he can elevate everybody around him. I played with Mahomes during his first three seasons, and what I see now is already a different man despite it only being a few years ago.

Mahomes is in command of the huddle, room, and building at all times. He plays through injury. He's the face of the NFL. He is somebody you can build around.

The Chiefs have done that in these years since the night in Tampa. And now, they're not going anywhere. ■

INTRODUCTION

The National Football League, at its core, is built upon hope.

The league prides itself on parity. All 32 owners agree that at the beginning of the season, every fan base should sincerely feel that its team has a chance to lift the Lombardi Trophy.

This is accomplished by a very intentional implementing of rules, such as the salary cap, limitations on franchise-tagged players, free agency, and the NFL Draft order — among others.

Consistently winning Super Bowl championships should be difficult. Every team in the league should go through phases in which they win more than lose, followed by phases in which they lose more than win.

Championships should be rare. Dynasties should be impossible.

In 2007, Kansas City Chiefs owner, chairman and CEO Clark Hunt went on record to say that he wanted his franchise to be more like that of the Pittsburgh Steelers, who can say they have had three head coaches in their rich history — a significant reason they have managed to raise six championship banners.

"I'm a strong believer that continuity at the head coaching position is very important to long-term success," said Hunt at the time. "Probably you could point to the Pittsburgh Steelers as the best example of that. They do a great job of drafting players, developing them, and playing them and they have tremendous continuity with their head coaches. They have a system and an approach about how they do it and it's important we develop that kind of mindset here."

Hunt's theory was correct, but the execution to follow failed, at least in his first attempt.

The era of Todd Haley and Scott Pioli did not lead to the type of shift in franchise direction for which Hunt was hoping. An eventual power struggle between general manager and head coach led to the partnership's demise. For well-known reasons both on and off the field, the Chiefs underwent their worst season ever in 2012, when they finished 2-14.

Hunt's second attempt at his theory changed the course of history — not only for his Chiefs, but also for the National Football League.

In 2013, Andy Reid became available after 14 seasons coaching the Philadelphia Eagles, a span that included four straight NFC Championship game trips and an NFC title.

The story is now Kansas City legend: Hunt secured Reid by meeting him at a Philadelphia airport, talking through their visions for hours, and ensuring that Reid did not board flights to Arizona or San Diego, where he was scheduled to meet the Cardinals and Chargers.

"I had been in the league a while, so I had known the family before I came here," said Reid. "I've said this before which is true, I sat in those owner meetings and there were just some people I looked at and I'd go, 'Boy, if something ever happened, I'm working for a great owner (Jeffrey Lurie), but if something ever happened here, I could see myself working for those people. They are just good people.'

"The Hunts were one of those families. I knew Clark, I knew his dad and I'm not going to say it was a no-brainer because you've got to think about everything, but I already had the answers to the test kind of just by knowing them."

About nine days after Hunt hired Reid, he hired

John Dorsey — the longtime Packers' talent evaluator who had worked with Reid in the mid-to-late 1990s — as the team's new general manager.

Learning from the failures of his previous regime, Hunt created a unique organizational hierarchy in which both Reid and Dorsey would report directly to him — as would team president Mark Donovan.

Reid and Dorsey overturned the roster in 2013, trading for Alex Smith, once again giving the Chiefs stability at the quarterback position, something it lacked since the days of Trent Green. Dorsey drafted Travis Kelce — and discovered "The Magnificent Seven," a group of key players who were made available during that year's 53-man roster deadline. Kansas City had its new foundation.

The organization's culture had instantly changed for the better under Reid. From 1998 to 2012, Kansas City made three playoff appearances. From 2013 to 2017, they made four.

But it was not enough for Hunt. Playoff games were great, but he wanted his team to bring home the Lamar Hunt Trophy — the prize named after his father awarded to the AFC Champions. Hunt wanted Super Bowl championships.

In the offseason following the 2017 season, Hunt made another difficult decision by saying goodbye to Dorsey for a homegrown Reid personnel executive: Brett Veach.

Veach started his career as Reid's coaching intern in Philadelphia in 2004, followed Reid to Kansas City as a personnel analyst in 2013 and had been the co-director of player personnel prior to his promotion to general manager.

To this day, Reid credits Veach with finding quarterback Patrick Mahomes, the Texas Tech product who had bad mechanics and threw from too many different arm angles. Dorsey executed the surprise trade-up with the Buffalo Bills on draft night.

Nobody — not even Hunt — understood what had just taken place. In a mere moment's time, Kansas City's franchise had changed forever.

In domino fashion, Hunt's decision-making to bring in Reid had led to the Chiefs drafting one of the greatest quarterbacks of all time. And over the years to follow, Veach's sharp eye for college talent and reconstruction of the team's cap strategy, has led to a supporting cast with whom Mahomes could win championships.

And that is what the Chiefs have done.

Mahomes became the first Chief in history to win the NFL MVP award in 2018, a feat he repeated in 2022. The Chiefs became the first team in history to host five conference championship games, and they won three AFC Championships.

With their Super Bowl LVII victory over the Philadelphia Eagles, they have won two Super Bowl championships in the last four seasons — and they have pieces in place to remain a contender for years to come.

A dynasty has begun. ■

Chiefs 38, Eagles 35
February 12, 2023 • Glendale, Arizona

'THE BEST FEELING IN THE WORLD'

Chiefs Regroup During Extended Halftime, Capture Second Title in Four Years

The Kansas City Chiefs entered the halftime locker room of Super Bowl LVII having been outgained, outscored, and outplayed through two quarters of football.

Doubted ahead of the game due to a lingering shoulder issue, Philadelphia Eagles quarterback Jalen Hurts showed no sign of injury, running for 63 yards and two touchdowns, and throwing for 183 yards and another touchdown in the first half alone. The Chiefs' youthful defensive backs were overwhelmed by the Eagles' star receivers, as the duo of A.J. Brown and DeVonta Smith combined for 129 yards.

Meanwhile, quarterback Patrick Mahomes and the Kansas City offense struggled to get anything going after tight end Travis Kelce scored on the initial drive of the game. Harrison Butker doinked a 42-yard field goal off the upright, and the Chiefs punted on back-to-back possessions to end the second quarter.

Had it not been for linebacker Nick Bolton's 36-yard scoop-and-score on Hurts' only real blemish of the game — a second-quarter fumble on a ball he simply dropped during a quarterback draw — it may have been much worse.

Still, trailing 24-14, the Chiefs realized if something did not change, they would be Super Bowl losers for the second time in four seasons. An extended break due to the yearly half-time show sounded as though it was just what the doctor ordered.

"The big difference between the first half and the second half was just energy," Kansas City wide receiver JuJu Smith-Schuster said after the game. "That 29 minutes was perfect. I didn't get to see the Rihanna performance — she was probably amazing, but that 29 minutes that we had literally brought us together."

One might think that it would have been Mahomes to stand in front of the room in an attempt to rally the troops, but it wasn't only him who spoke up.

"It was everybody," said the quarterback after the game. "It wasn't like I was the only person talking in that locker room. We just challenged each other to leave everything out there, and I don't want to say we played tight in the first half, but you didn't see that same joy that we play with. I wanted guys to just know that everything we've worked for is for this moment. You have to enjoy this moment. You can't let the moment overtake you, and I thought the guys did that in the

Defensive end Carlos Dunlap celebrates with the Lombardi Trophy after defeating the Philadelphia Eagles 38-35 in Super Bowl LVII.

second half and they fought to the very end."

The Chiefs received the ball to start the third quarter, and they looked like an entirely different team. Kansas City head coach Andy Reid leaned back into rookie Isiah Pacheco, Jerick McKinnon, and the run game — and Mahomes began to get Smith-Schuster more involved. Pacheco, who ran for 76 yards on 15 carries for the day, scored a touchdown from one yard out to cut the Eagles' lead to three.

The Chiefs' defense regained some confidence on the next drive when they were finally able to hold Philadelphia to three points after they had converted three third downs and a fourth down. On third-and-11 at the Kansas City 20-yard line, Bolton made a pivotal open-field tackle of running back Kenneth Gainwell, and head coach Nick Sirianni sent on his field goal unit.

Behind six points, Mahomes and the Chiefs marched back onto the field, picking up where they left off from the previous possession. Mahomes found Smith-Schuster four times for 38 yards on the drive, as part of a 53-yard day for Smith-Schuster. The play led Kansas City inside the 10-yard line.

Reid then called on wide receiver Kadarius Toney, who had battled an ankle injury of his own to be active for the game. Toney faked a jet sweep before stopping in his tracks to leak into the flat, where he was wide open. Mahomes delivered the ball to him for the score. Out of nowhere, the Chiefs had a 28-27 lead early in the fourth quarter.

The Kansas City defense forced a three-and-out, and Philadelphia lined up to punt. As it turned out, Toney was not done making an impact on the big stage. With a flair for the dramatic, Toney caught the ball low before reversing to the opposite sideline and darting up the field for a 65-yard gain.

The Chiefs were at the Eagles' 5-yard line, and a play later, Reid called a similar-looking play to the one that Toney scored on, but this time, rookie Skyy Moore

Tight end Travis Kelce catches an 18-yard pass ahead of Eagles safety Marcus Epps for the Chiefs' first touchdown of the night.

was wide open. Moore's first career touchdown came in the Super Bowl.

"They were different plays; they were good," said Reid. "My assistant coaches are unbelievable. Eric Bieniemy with the game plan and to coordinate the thing and the young guys — all these young guys I got contribute. They've all got their spot in which they put plays in — Greg Lewis, David Girardi — they all added plays in there, and heck, they all work. They never tell me which one doesn't, but these plays show up."

Suddenly, the Eagles were the team on the ropes, down 35-27 with a little more than nine minutes left in the game. Hurts did not flinch. At the Kansas City 47, Hurts connected on a pass to Smith for a gain of 45 yards, putting him in a position to record his third rushing touchdown of the game. Hurts followed his blocks on the next play to complete the two-point conversion.

Thanks to Hurts — who finished 27-of-38 for 304 yards and a touchdown, as well as 15 carries for 70 yards and three rushing touchdowns — Super Bowl LVII was tied at 35 with four minutes to go. Mahomes, who was 21-of-27 for 182 yards and three touchdowns, needed one more scoring drive to get it done.

Facing a third-and-1 at midfield, Pacheco busted it outside for a gain of 10, into Philadelphia territory. On the next play, Mahomes stepped up and scrambled through the Eagles' defense for 26 yards. The Chiefs had the ball in the red zone with just over two minutes to play.

"They did a good job of covering the guys I wanted to throw to," Mahomes said of the play. "That was the biggest thing, and I got going upfield and how the D-line rushed, it left a lane... you just try and get into field-goal range. We have a great kicker and you want to give him a chance to kick a field goal or score a touchdown."

With time winding down, the Eagles used their second timeout, leading to a third down. Mahomes targeted Smith-Schuster, but the ball fell to the turf. However, so too did a penalty flag. Philadelphia cornerback James Bradberry had been called for holding. First down Kansas City.

Jalen Hurts fumbles the ball in the second quarter, one of the Eagles quarterback's only mishaps of the game. Chiefs linebacker Nick Bolton took full advantage on the play with a 36-yard scoop-and-score.

Mahomes handed it off to McKinnon on the next play, and he took it to the 2 before sliding right before the goal line. Two kneels set up a 27-yard field goal for Harrison Butker, which he drilled through the uprights.

The Chiefs led the Eagles 38-35 with eight seconds left on the clock. A Hurts heave later, and Kansas City had a world champion.

"It's the greatest feeling in the world," Kelce said after the game. "Being here with the guys that we did it with, with the coaches we did it with, through all the adversity, there's nothing I could say that could really explain how I'm feeling right now.

"Being at the top with my brothers and teammates is the best feeling in the world." ◾

Above: Kansas City Chiefs head coach Andy Reid celebrates with Travis Kelce after the win. Opposite: Rookie running back Isiah Pacheco scores a one-yard touchdown early in the third quarter to cut into the Eagles' lead.

Place kicker Harrison Butker kicks the game winning field goal against the Philadelphia Eagles to cap the thrilling 38-35 victory.

KANSAS CITY CHIEFS VS PHILADELPHIA EAGLES

RISING TO THE OCCASION

Patrick Mahomes Captures Second Super Bowl MVP in Gutsy Performance

Three nights after winning his second Most Valuable Player award for the entirety of the 2022 NFL season, Kansas City Chiefs quarterback Patrick Mahomes had his second Super Bowl MVP.

Mahomes finished the Super Bowl 21-of-27 for 182 yards and three touchdowns, adding a remarkable 44 yards on six carries despite a high-ankle sprain he suffered in the team's Divisional Round win over the Jacksonville Jaguars.

It appeared that Mahomes may have even re-injured the ankle late in the second quarter as he was tackled by linebacker T.J. Edwards.

"It felt great until I kind of rolled it a little bit," he said after the game. "I felt really good, and then that happened. A lot of soreness going through into halftime, and I was able to move it around, get taped up a little bit and go out there in the second half. It felt good, but I was going to leave it all out there. I'm glad that it was enough for the win."

Mahomes' night started out strong, as he executed a touchdown drive in six plays on the opening possession. Seeing his favorite target, tight end Travis Kelce, had one-on-one coverage, Mahomes floated a pass 18 yards down the field for an over-the-shoulder touchdown.

Mahomes and the Chiefs' offense went through mid-game lull before he would add wide-open touchdowns to wide receivers Kadarius Toney and Skyy Moore in the fourth quarter.

"He grew up in a locker room," said head coach Andy Reid of his quarterback after the game. "He's seen the greats, and he strives to be the greatest. Without saying anything, that's the way he works. He wants to be the greatest player ever. That's what he wants to do, and that's the way he goes about his business. And he does it humbly. There's no bragging. He can stand up here and give you these stats that are incredible that he's had, but he's never going to do that. That's just not him, and so we appreciate that.

"When it's time for the guys around them to raise their game, he helps them with that. The great quarterbacks make everybody around them better, including the head coach. So he's done a heck of a job."

Mahomes' most important plays of the night may have come on scrambles as he nursed his re-aggravated right ankle.

First, early in the third quarter, a 14-yard run set up an Isiah Pacheco touchdown to turn the tide in favor of the Chiefs. Then, with three minutes to go and the game tied at 35, Mahomes scrambled 26 yards up the field to get Kansas City in field-goal range.

Harrison Butker would hit a 27-yard field goal to put the Chiefs up 38-35 for good. With a three-touchdown performance, Mahomes had a second title — and Super Bowl MVP award.

"It hasn't even sunk in I don't think even yet," said Mahomes. "I appreciate it because of the failures — the failures of losing a Super Bowl and then losing an AFC Championship game. It gives you a greater appreciation to be standing here as a champion.

"Luckily, I'm going to Disneyland now, so I have Disneyland and Disney World crossed off, and they'll have to make some more parks so I can go around them everywhere and do a world tour." ∎

Patrick Mahomes hoists the Lombardi Trophy after the Chiefs secured their second Super Bowl win in four years. Mahomes was also awarded his second Super Bowl MVP award.

ROAD TO THE
SUPER BOWL

IT'S MY 7th
BIRTHDAY

HOYT

PLEASE SIGN MY CARD

CHANGING OF THE GUARD

GM Brett Veach Shuffles the Deck with Another Championship in Mind

Reaching the ultimate goal in the National Football League — winning a Super Bowl — comes with a rush of simultaneous diametrically opposed emotions.

On one hand, a team has accomplished the unthinkable — overcoming obstacles, injury, and adversity to defeat the best in the world en route to the mountaintop. Looking back, so many circumstances had to go a particular way for dreams to become a reality. The road seems unrepeatable.

Yet, at the same time, the ungraspable has been grasped, hasn't it? If that same team brings back the core pieces — the quarterback, the head coach, and most of the staff members — couldn't they do it again?

Couldn't they "run it back?"

In the years after his Super Bowl LIV victory, on several occasions, Kansas City Chiefs quarterback Patrick Mahomes openly talked about how 2018 and 2019 all seemed so easy to come by. And in retrospect, maybe too easy. At the age of 24, he was the 2018 AP NFL MVP. He was a Super Bowl LIV MVP and champion.

The 2020 Super Bowl LV loss and 2021 AFC Championship loss taught him the importance of smelling the roses.

"I think when I first got in the league it all happened so fast," recalled Mahomes after clinching the 2022 AFC Championship. "I won the MVP; I won the Super Bowl and I thought that's just kind of how it went. You were going to play, I listened to what coach Reid said and that stuff happens and now that I've dealt with failure and losing the AFC Championship and losing the Super Bowl, I know how much hard work and daily grind that it takes."

And not only does it take work; it also takes terribly tough-but-necessary decisions.

During the 2022 offseason, following the Chiefs' loss to the Cincinnati Bengals in the AFC championship, general manager Brett Veach had to say goodbye to some of the most important individuals in the history of the Chiefs' franchise.

And had those decisions not been made, it's difficult to believe the Chiefs would have been able to accomplish winning a Super Bowl title for the second time in four seasons.

Chiefs trade wide receiver Tyreek Hill to the Miami Dolphins

Trading a three-time, first-team All-Pro with 7,349 regular-season scrimmage yards and 62 total regular-season touchdowns, as well as 1,172 playoff scrimmage yards and six total playoff touchdowns takes some guts.

In return from the Miami Dolphins, the Chiefs

Chiefs general manager Brett Veach signs autographs for fans after the Chiefs' win over the Cincinnati Bengals in the AFC championship game. Following the Chiefs' loss to the Bengals in the AFC championship game a year earlier, Veach made a number of key personnel moves to help the Chiefs return to the Super Bowl.

received five future picks in the NFL Draft, including a first-round pick in 2022. They saved more than $70 million worth of cap space.

Hill had more than 1,300 scrimmage yards for the Chiefs in 2021, which means Veach would have to bring in new weapons for quarterback Patrick Mahomes.

Ahead of the 2022 season, the Chiefs signed receivers JuJu Smith-Schuster, Marquez Valdes-Scantling, Justin Watson, and drafted Skyy Moore out of Western Michigan with the No. 54 overall pick in the second round of the draft.

Smith-Schuster spent the first five years of his career in Pittsburgh and Valdes-Scantling spent the first four years in Green Bay. Neither managed a ring despite their time with future Pro Football Hall of Fame quarterbacks.

That would change in Kansas City.

Chiefs let safety Tyrann Mathieu walk, sign Justin Reid

The Chiefs signed safety Tyrann Mathieu ahead of the 2019 season to fill a key leadership role left vacant by the release of Eric Berry. Mathieu would coin the phrase, "championship swagger," and he lived it, with not only his own play, but also how he would bring others up.

Throughout the 2021 NFL season, Mathieu made it clear he wanted to remain with the Chiefs, but Veach chose to let "Honey Badger" go, reportedly never making an offer.

In March, the Chiefs signed safety Justin Reid, who had spent the first four years of his career as a member of the Houston Texans.

Much like Mathieu, Reid was a do-it-all safety who could play on the line, in the box, as a slot cornerback, an outside cornerback and as a free safety. Reid projected as someone who could be a leader for the club, just like his predecessor.

Mathieu signed with the New Orleans Saints.

Chiefs cut linebacker Anthony Hitchens, turning room over to Nick Bolton

Much like Mathieu, linebacker Anthony Hitchens was pivotal to Kansas City's Super Bowl title.

Hitchens actually signed with the Chiefs a year before Mathieu, in 2018. Bringing Hitchens to the Chiefs was one of Veach's first significant roster moves after he was promoted to the role of general manager.

The man whom Chiefs defensive coordinator Steve Spagnuolo called the "glue" of the Chiefs' defense, Hitchens helped lead the Chiefs to four straight AFC title games, two AFC championships and the Super Bowl LIV title.

To Hitchens' credit, despite knowing that the 2021 rookie progress of Nick Bolton would likely mean the end of his Chiefs' tenure, he worked diligently to prepare him and teach him the MIKE linebacker role.

Bolton talks about Hitchens with reverence to this day, acknowledging how much of a role he played in his growth. ∎

Nick Bolton gestures to Chiefs Kingdom as the team takes the field before a January 2023 game against the Denver Broncos. After the Chiefs cut linebacker Anthony Hitchens, Bolton took on the important MIKE linebacker role.

QUARTERBACK

PATRICK MAHOMES

Mahomes and KC Offense Take a New Approach with 'Camp Pat'

The Kansas City Chiefs understood what trading a generational wide receiver such as Tyreek Hill would mean when it came to their offense — it would take time for quarterback Patrick Mahomes to gel with his new pass-catchers.

So when Phase One of the offseason program began for the Chiefs in April, head coach Andy Reid broke a routine he's had for years, allowing for something completely unorthodox.

While the Chiefs *could* return to their facility in Kansas City to work out and meet with coaches off the field, they *didn't* — at least for players on the offensive side of the football. Instead, many reported to Mahomes' home state of Texas, working out there and meeting with Reid and the rest of the coaching staff virtually.

"I think the biggest thing for the work we've been getting in Texas is, first, we want to build those relationships," explained Mahomes. "I think that's what made us so great over these last few years is we have a team — the bond of our team, the chemistry that we have, that we can go out there and be who we are. So I wanted to get everybody together, so they get to meet each other."

Beginning in 2017, Mahomes' supporting cast had mostly been the same. Sure, Hill and tight end Travis Kelce made up the core of the offense, but Demarcus Robinson had been a contributor since 2016, and Byron Pringle had been with the club since 2018.

Both Robinson and Pringle were no longer with the club.

A lot of new faces would be learning the offense from scratch, so why not get a head start?

Mahomes not only invited the big-name acquisitions, such as wide receivers JuJu Smith-Schuster and Marquez Valdes-Scantling. Role players like wide receiver Justin Watson and running back Ronald Jones earned a call.

Learning Reid's verbiage helps from some expert guidance, reasoned the quarterback.

"They learn how each other act with each other and how to build those friendships," said Mahomes. "I wanted to really focus on the details because you get to start brand new again... those things that you kind of just blew through and went through really quickly last year — you get to really focus on those details, which I

Following the offseason departures of receiver Tyreek Hill and other key contributors, Patrick Mahomes gelled with a new cast of pass-catchers in 2022.

think is a great thing for us because we'll get to go back to the basics of it, learn it from there and then evolve as the season goes on."

During Phase One, the Chiefs' coaches cannot instruct players on the field, anyway, so Reid uncharacteristically decided it would be best to break a years-long tradition.

"We're going to meet with them virtually," explained Reid. "There's a number of guys that are here lifting, but again, these are all voluntary camps — all three phases. But they'll be able to work out on their own and do that part. We've had some gatherings with some of the skill players offensively — Pat organized some guys that are down in Texas with him and they're throwing to a couple new receivers that we have. [They're] down there with him along with the rest of the skill players — new running backs, etc. It's moving in a positive direction. Look forward to getting these meetings started as we go forward."

In Kansas City, Reid said the Chiefs would handle the "football part" of things. In the afternoon, coaches would evaluate draft prospect film.

Meanwhile, Reid counted on Mahomes to ensure the current players get in the proper work.

"That's where I have the trust in the guys to be able to do this with the virtual," said the head coach. "We don't need them right here. We've played a lot of games in the last four to five years — maybe more than anyone in the National Football League, so having them with a little time away to do their bonding with themselves, especially with the influx of new players, I think is important, and then, when they get here, they'll be revved up. And we'll be in this building for quite a time, so these two weeks though, that they can really be with themselves, working and getting to know each other, I think is important."

Mahomes further explained how Phase One shifted from a workout program in Kansas City to a makeshift training camp of sorts in Texas.

"It kind of started off where I was going to have some guys come run routes and do stuff like that before OTAs started, and then, as I kind of talked to coach Reid and [Eric Bieniemy], they informed me, they were like, 'If you want to get everybody down there, then we can do the virtual these first few weeks, and kind of keep everybody together.'"

Returners to the club, such as Mecole Hardman, also took part in "Camp Pat."

"It's going good," explained Hardman. "Just basic terminology, getting our feet wet, knocking the rust off a little bit and getting some timing down and trying to get prepared before we get to OTAs."

Mahomes liked the fact that he was getting to know his new targets better off the field.

"I'm going to lunch with these guys," he said. "I'm working out with these guys as well — not just throwing. So you kind of build those relationships that way. And then, plus, we're in a little warmer weather than KC is right now, so it was a thing where we were going to have to work, anyway, and get off the field. We decided as long as we were in Texas working together, the coaches said that we could do it virtually and still get the learning that we need.

"It involves the trust that they have in us that we're going to be vets and we're going to do it the right way like we've been doing. And whenever we roll into KC in May, we'll be ready to go then, too." ■

Patrick Mahomes led the Chiefs to the AFC championship for the third time in 2022.

LENNY THE COOL

Chiefs Pay Tribute to Franchise Legend Len Dawson

In late August, Kansas City Chiefs legend Len Dawson died at the age of 87.

Dawson's family issued an official statement.

"With wife Linda at his side, it is with much sadness that we inform you of the passing of our beloved Len Dawson. He was a wonderful husband, father, brother, and friend. Len was always grateful, and many times overwhelmed by the countless bonds he made during his football and broadcast careers.

"He loved Kansas City and no matter where his travels took him, he could not wait to return home.

"Linda wants to acknowledge and thank the wonderful team of doctors, nurses and support staff at KU Med who showed tremendous amounts of love and compassion for Len."

Kansas City's first great quarterback led the Chiefs to the first ever Super Bowl, and then went on to win Super Bowl IV in 1970. Dawson retired from football following the 1975 season but would continue his involvement in the game as a KMBC9 broadcaster and color analyst on the Chiefs Radio Network.

He was inducted into the Pro Football Hall of Fame in 1987 and his No. 16 is one of the 11 jersey numbers retired by the franchise.

The Chiefs' first game following the announcement of Dawson's death took place on Thursday night, August 25 — the final preseason matchup of the year, as the Chiefs hosted the Green Bay Packers.

Before the game began, the team announced players would wear a No. 16 decal on their helmets all season, including the playoffs and Super Bowl LVII, should they make it that far.

On the team's first offensive possession, quarterback Patrick Mahomes came up with his own special way to honor Dawson.

Mahomes was not expected to play much, given it was the team's final preseason game, so it was a bit of a surprise to see him march out onto the field with the offense.

As it turned out, Mahomes had no intention to snap the football. He instead gathered his unit in just the fashion Dawson would in the 1960s: in a "choir" huddle.

"That was Clark [Hunt's] suggestion and players completely bought into it and wanted to do it — and then we added just the little wrinkle at the end there," said Chiefs head coach Andy Reid after the team's 17-10 win.

Referee Craig Wrolstad called the delay-of-game penalty on "Kansas City, No. 16."

"The official did an amazing job of mentioning Len," continued Reid. "It's a tribute to a great person, a great player and then all he did in [broadcast journalism] there. Very seldom are you a Hall of Famer in two different things. He had a wonderful life and really took advantage of every day he had on Earth here."

Mahomes, who developed a relationship with Dawson since the team drafted him in 2017, explained that he and his teammates wanted to figure out a special way to honor him.

"I think Clark and coach Reid talked about it, and they came up with the idea," said Mahomes. "And obviously, we're praying for his family, but he did so

Len Dawson gets set to take a snap during Super Bowl IV in 1970. The legendary Chiefs quarterback and broadcaster passed away in August 2022 at the age of 87.

much to impact the Kansas City community and this organization. We wanted to do something, a little token to show our appreciation and I'm glad we got to do it out here at GEHA Field at Arrowhead."

The Chiefs have had many starting quarterbacks over the years, but only two who were able to bring home a title: Mahomes and Dawson.

"He was a part of that great group that made the Chiefs who we are today," said Mahomes. "So, he started off there and as a broadcaster, calling the games. I think a lot of people grew up listening to Len talking and broadcasting those games. And as a person, he was one of the best people that I've met, and I got to meet him a couple of times here. He always had advice for me on how to embrace this community because it's such a great community."

Reid added that tight end Travis Kelce — like Mahomes — was not scheduled to play. But Kelce insisted that he should be on the field for the tribute.

"He wanted to jump in there," said Reid of Kelce. "And then the defense couldn't wait to see it. It was crazy, the way it worked out. [Defensive coordinator Steve Spagnuolo], he missed it. And he was the guy who was most excited about it, and he missed it over there talking to his guys. But he'll see it on tape there. It was a neat deal. Again, for a great person."

After the delay of game, Mahomes jogged off the field to an ovation from those in the stands. It is likely a moment he won't soon forget.

"It's special," said Mahomes. "I mean there is only a certain amount of quarterbacks who get to win Super Bowls. Len kind of set the standard here in Kansas City, and I'm thankful enough to be able to go up there and win one. It's hard to do.

"I think I realize that every year playing. It's hard to do, to win a Super Bowl. I'm going to try and do my best to get more flags up there and try to win a few more Super Bowls." ∎

As a tribute to Len Dawson, Patrick Mahomes and the Chiefs' offensive players stood in a choir huddle during a preseason game against the Packers.

Chiefs 44, Cardinals 21
September 11, 2022 • Glendale, Arizona

BEGINNING AT THE END

Chiefs Vanquish Cards in First Step to Super Bowl LVII

Fresh off a splashy offseason decision to move their wildly popular, three-time All-Pro wide receiver, Tyreek Hill, the Kansas City Chiefs began their 2022 campaign where they hoped it would end: State Farm Stadium in Phoenix, Arizona, home of the Arizona Cardinals and Super Bowl LVII.

Coming into the year, any offseason chatter relating to the Chiefs included how they would manage without Hill, who had accounted for more than 7,000 scrimmage yards and 62 touchdowns during his six-year tenure in Kansas City.

Throughout training camp, quarterback Patrick Mahomes frequently said that in 2022, the production would come from "everywhere." Against his former college coach from Texas Tech, Kliff Kingsbury — and the Cardinals — he made a statement in his first regular-season opportunity, targeting 10 different receivers to the tune of 360 yards and five touchdowns in a 44-21 Chiefs win.

"I think guys were just ready to go," said Mahomes. "They're excited to get out there and show what we had. All offseason everyone has asked us questions of what this team would look like and we've always believed that we were going to go out there and put on a show and I thought guys did that. So to go out there and win against a really good football team and to win decisively, it's a good start."

During a year in which he promised to spread the ball around, the recipient of Mahomes' first touchdown of the season was his most usual suspect: tight end Travis Kelce. Pressured in the pocket, Mahomes floated a 7-yard pass over the head of linebacker Isiah Simmons.

Kelce served his quarterback reliably, leading Kansas City with eight catches for 121 yards and a touchdown, as his score was the first strike as part of a 37-7 run to start the game. Wide receiver JuJu Smith-Schuster, brought in by the Chiefs to help fill the void left by Hill, was next in receiving with six catches for 79 yards.

"I think with Pat today, he kind of gave me a taste of what it feels like to be on the football field with him," said the Chiefs' wide receiver. "Moving around... he created extra time. I feel like a lot of our first downs were created because of Patrick moving his legs."

Running back Clyde Edwards-Helaire caught two touchdown passes in the win.

The Cardinals' only glimmer of hope came from a second-quarter fumble by Smith-Schuster recovered by Cardinals cornerback Byron Murphy. At the time, the Cardinals only trailed the Chiefs, 14-7. But despite beginning their drive at the Kansas City 42, the Cardinals could not take advantage, turning the football over on downs four plays later.

Led by safety Juan Thornhill, who had a near-interception as part of two total pass breakups, Chiefs

Running back Jerick McKinnon and the Kansas City offense ran roughshod over the Cardinals, with 488 total yards and 44 points in the easy win.

defensive coordinator Steve Spagnuolo's unit may have played just as well as the offense. The Chiefs made Cardinals quarterback Kyler Murray uncomfortable throughout the game, hitting him four times and only allowing only 29 rushing yards. Defensive end Carlos Dunlap, defensive tackle Turk Wharton and cornerback L'Jarius Sneed had a sack apiece as the Chiefs recorded seven passes defensed.

The Cardinals entered the game undermanned, missing defensive end JJ Watt and wide receivers DeAndre Hopkins and Rondale Moore. Still, the Chiefs left the game with availability issues of their own.

As a result of turf issues at State Farm Stadium, Kansas City saw two key players go down with injuries: kicker Harrison Butker and rookie first-rounder Trent McDuffie. Butker rolled his ankle as he kicked the ball off following the Chiefs' first touchdown, and McDuffie pulled his hamstring.

"It was a little bit loose," said head coach Andy Reid the next week. "That's what happens you know sometimes when you re-sod it, it's loose...it was part of the Butker injury and McDuffie injury."

The move by the Chiefs to add safety Justin Reid in the offseason as a replacement for Tyrann Mathieu paid dividends right away, but not exactly as Kansas City had expected. Once Butker rolled his ankle, Reid hit the next extra point, the equivalent of a 33-yarder — and on kickoffs, was exploding through the ball for touchbacks.

"We may need to talk about putting some incentives in there," laughed the safety. "I had a ton of fun out there. It threw me back to my high school days just being out there and having fun."

After receiving medical attention, Butker reentered the game to miraculously connect on a 54-yarder using a one-step run-up, but he would miss the next four games. McDuffie would miss the next six.

Butker and McDuffie may have hoped at the time to never see State Farm Stadium again.

Of course, they'd be back. ∎

Rookie running back Isiah Pacheco had a strong NFL debut with 12 carries for 62 yards and a touchdown.

Chiefs 27, Chargers 24

September 15, 2022 • Kansas City, Missouri

REASON TO CELEBRATE

Chiefs Fight Through Quick Thursday Turnaround, Get Past Rival Chargers

The 2022 NFL season marked the first year of partnership between the NFL and Amazon, who agreed to a deal with the league to take over Thursday Night Football broadcasts. Months ahead of the season, the league's premier scribe and insider, Peter King, reported that Amazon wanted to debut their new acquisition with a game at GEHA Field at Arrowhead Stadium, given the "star power" of Kansas City Chiefs quarterback Patrick Mahomes.

And while Mahomes performed efficiently in the game, throwing for 235 yards and two touchdowns in a 27-24 victory over the Los Angeles Chargers, it was a seventh-round rookie, Jaylen Watson, who gave the fans watching worldwide a show. Watson started because first-round rookie Trent McDuffie was placed on injured reserve with a severe hamstring injury.

With the game tied at 17 midway through the third quarter, Chargers quarterback Justin Herbert had his team with first-and-goal at the Kansas City 3. Looking to his right, Herbert saw that tight end Gerald Everett would be one-on-one with Watson, a favorable matchup considering it featured a sixth-year veteran pass-catcher against a rookie making his first career start.

Herbert tried to find Everett, but Watson jumped the pass for the interception, taking the ball 99 yards to the opposite end zone for the score.

"Me and Justin [Reid], we worked together," said Watson. "The ball just ended up in my chest and I took it home. It was a surreal feeling. [I'm] just so grateful and blessed to be in this position. I didn't even know what to do when I got in the end zone... everyone [saw] me just standing there. But, it's a moment I'll never forget."

Watson's pick-six — the longest go-ahead fourth-quarter touchdown scored by a rookie in NFL history — gave the Chiefs a 24-17 lead. Then, after exchanging three straight punts, Kansas City replacement kicker Matt Ammendola extended it to 27-17, important points, as the Chargers would score a late-game touchdown.

On the Monday before *Thursday Night Football,* Ammendola won what had been described as a "six-man kicker derby" run by Chiefs special teams coordinator Dave Toub. Ammendola, who had found himself out of the league after going 13 of 19 in his career, was a perfect 2-of-2 on field goals and 3-of-3 on extra points.

Undrafted in 2020, Ammendola found his fourth team in two years when he signed with the Chiefs.

"People bounce around from team to team, so you always kind of have to stay ready whether I'm back home or out in San Diego training," Ammendola said. "Harrison's been great. Tommy [Townsend], James [Winchester] have all been great help just getting me ready for tonight and obviously went out there and had

Cornerback Jaylen Watson's 99-yard interception return for a touchdown gave the Chiefs the lead for good in the win over the Chargers.

a great time with the guys and just happy to just really show out and make the most of the opportunity."

The Chargers built a 10-0 lead on the Chiefs with a 1-yard pass to fullback Zander Horvath early in the second quarter. After two empty possessions to start the game, Mahomes broke through on the next drive. Flushed to his right at the Los Angeles 9, he extended the play with his legs, allowing a sidearm toss to Jerick McKinnon.

The Chargers answered in the third quarter, as wide receiver Mike Williams — a rival well known for his strong performances against the Chiefs — astonishingly made a one-handed, 15-yard catch despite the blanket coverage of cornerback L'Jarius Sneed. The 15-yard grab added to a 113-yard night against the Chiefs.

Leading 17-7 in the third quarter, the Chargers were in control, and the game seemed like it could be over when cornerback Asante Samuel Jr. bounced a ball off his knee, dove in front of him and appeared to catch a Mahomes pass for a sure interception. After his official review, referee Walter Anderson explained that he saw the ball hit the ground.

The Chiefs' offensive drive stayed alive, allowing for Mahomes to connect with wide receiver Justin Watson six plays later. Watson shook off star cornerback J.C. Jackson to bring in a touchdown 41 yards down the field.

"It was just fun — we talked about that route in the receiver room," said the receiver after the game. "I wanted that route. Never want to see one of our receivers go down but (I) just want to give them the confidence that if they do have to take a play off the field that I am going to come in and do my job."

Watson the *receiver's* score led to Watson the cornerback's score, which led to a key change in team's off-the-field plans scheduled for that weekend.

Coincidentally, Watson *the cornerback* shares a September 17 birthday with Mahomes.

"I talked to [Watson] and I'm having a little birthday party on Saturday," smiled the quarterback, "so I said it's his birthday party now because of the way he played." ∎

Behind 235 yards and two touchdowns from Patrick Mahomes, the Chiefs improved to 2-0 on the season.

Colts 20, Chiefs 17

September 25, 2022 • Indianapolis, Indiana

UNSPORTSMANLIKE CONDUCT

Late Penalty Gives Colts New Life, Chiefs First Loss

Despite a lackluster performance from the offense and a mistake-filled afternoon for the special teams unit, the Kansas City Chiefs were in a position to win their third game in a row against the previously 0-1-1 Indianapolis Colts.

That was — until they weren't.

The Colts faced third-and-6 late in the fourth quarter, trailing the Chiefs 17-13. Colts quarterback Matt Ryan dropped back to find that defensive coordinator Steve Spagnuolo had called a blitz. Kansas City linebacker Nick Bolton ran through Indianapolis running back Nyheim Hines, meeting Ryan for a sack and what should have been a game-clinching play for the Chiefs.

But Chiefs defensive tackle Chris Jones had words for Ryan after the play, leading to an unsportsmanlike conduct penalty and giving the Colts a fresh set of downs at the 46-yard line. Ryan's march continued, and the drive eventually ended with a 12-yard go-ahead touchdown pass to tight end Jelani Woods. The Colts led 20-17. It was Woods' second score of the game.

In the locker room after the game, Jones said he had to do a better job at not talking to opposing teams.

"It sucks, man, because I blame myself for that," said Jones. "It was third down, we got off the field, defense fought hard, and I kind of put us in a situation to get back on the field. Then we got scored on, and that sums up the game. So, I'll take that one. It was my fault. It was definitely my fault. As a veteran player on this team, I have to be better with those types of things, especially in those situations. But it won't happen again from me. I take full blame. I apologize to my team for putting us in that type of situation. It was third down, we were off the field, (and) we would have given our offense the ball back."

The Chiefs' offense *did* get the ball back, but at their own 30-yard line with less than 20 seconds left on the clock. Mahomes looked for wide receiver JuJu Smith-Schuster, but the Colts deflected the pass, and it was intercepted by safety Rodney McLeod, ending the game.

Kansas City's offense appeared out of sync all day, with missed throws, dropped passes and an inability to consistently move the ball on the ground. The Chiefs quarterback was 20-of-35 for 262 yards, just one touchdown and the interception.

"It starts with me," said Mahomes. "There were certain throws I was putting on guys' back hips instead of in front of them. There were certain situations where we were just barely off — whether it was a defensive lineman [that] got around my feet and I missed Justin Watson, or it was a throw at the end of the game where I could've tried to put in front of JuJu and it gets tipped up for a pick. It's just little things like that."

The offense did manage two touchdowns, a receiving touchdown for tight end Travis Kelce and a rushing touchdown for running back Clyde Edwards-Helaire, but the special teams woes were too much to overcome. It might have been the worst special teams performance under the supervision of coordinator Dave Toub.

The Chiefs limited star running back Jonathan Taylor to 71 yards on 21 carries but couldn't hold on for the road win

To start the game, rookie wide receiver Skyy Moore muffed two punts — one of which led to Woods' first touchdown after beginning their offensive drive at Kansas City's 4-yard line.

Following a dependable Week 2 outing, replacement kicker Matt Ammendola missed an extra point on the next drive, causing the Chiefs to go for two after their next touchdown. After making a 26-yarder, Ammendola missed from 34 in the fourth quarter — which made head coach Andy Reid and Toub later call a fake field-goal attempt. The Chiefs also had a delay-of-game penalty called on a field goal.

"In the NFL, the parity is crazy, so any mistakes get magnified, and that's just how it goes," said Reid. "We have to clean that up. We have to clean it up. We'll get that taken care of."

The Chiefs' offense and special teams failed a strong performance by the defense, which played admirably in their first of four games without suspended linebacker Willie Gay Jr. Star running back Jonathan Taylor was held to 71 yards on 21 carries, and Ryan was sacked five times, including two from Bolton.

The Chiefs would have a *new* new kicker the following Tuesday. ∎

Chiefs 41, Buccaneers 31
October 2, 2022 • Tampa, Florida

'HOUDINI' ESCAPES WITH A WIN

Kansas City Gets Super Bowl Revenge, Quiets Tampa Bay

Given the success of Kansas City football over the past half-decade, the Chiefs don't typically begin a season with many "revenge" games circled on their calendar. The thought process invoked by Andy Reid is that every day — and every matchup — matters.

That mindset may be the key component to the head coach's consistency: his players' emotions hardly ever get too high or too low. However, on occasion, that principle works way better in theory than reality.

In Week 4 of the NFL season, amid a hurricane scare that threatened to move the *Sunday Night Football* game to Minnesota, the Chiefs traveled down to the site of their Super Bowl LV loss, Tampa, to face the Buccaneers, who chose to wear the same white uniforms they wore in that Super Bowl, as they started the same quarterback: Tom Brady.

In *theory,* it was just another game for the Chiefs. In *reality,* they wanted to right a wrong.

And if that wasn't motivation enough, Buccaneers linebacker Shaq Barrett decided to insult Kansas City on a Zoom meeting with Tampa Bay media heading into the game.

In Super Bowl LV, the Chiefs were without several starters along their offensive line, including tackles Eric Fisher and Mitch Schwartz. On that night, Barrett took advantage, hitting Chiefs quarterback Patrick Mahomes four times and sacking him once as the Buccaneers rolled to a 31-9 championship victory.

Spearheading one of the NFL's top defenses through three weeks of the 2022 season, Barrett used that memory to jeer the offensive line rebuilt by general manager Brett Veach with the additions of Orlando Brown Jr., Joe Thuney, Creed Humphrey, and Trey Smith.

"I really don't think [the offensive line is] too much of a difference," laughed the linebacker. "I think we have a lot of favorable matchups. I think we really have an opportunity to really dominate the game... I just think, yeah, we've got an opportunity to really impose our will as pass-rushers, edge rushers in this game. We can really have like a coming-out party."

The Chiefs appeared as though they heard the noise as early as the opening kickoff, when they forced and recovered a Rachaad White fumble, with cornerback Chris Lammons knocking the ball away and linebacker Elijah Lee there to land on the football.

Despite kicking off, Kansas City began on offense at Tampa Bay's 21-yard line. Mahomes quickly took advantage of the short field, finding tight end Travis Kelce for his third touchdown of the season.

Cornerback L'Jarius Sneed (38) sacks Tom Brady and forces a fumble in the 41-31 shootout win.

Only 46 seconds into the game, Kelce danced in Tampa Bay's end zone.

Behind their offensive line, the Chiefs marched right back down the field the next drive, all the way to the Tampa Bay 3. Taking a handoff from fellow running back Jerick McKinnon, Clyde Edwards-Helaire followed the goal-line push of Thuney and Humphrey, and Brown got behind Edwards-Helaire, driving him to break the plane and extend the Chiefs' lead to 14-3 late in the first quarter.

The Buccaneers went three-and-out, allowing for Mahomes and company to continue pouring it on. Facing second-and-goal, Mahomes felt the head and bailed out to his right. He broke a tackle, spun around 360 degrees, and flicked a pass that dropped perfectly into the hands of Edwards-Helaire to give the Chiefs a 21-3 lead.

With Brady being the league's consensus "G.O.A.T.," Mahomes needed a new nickname.

"He's the Houdini of our era," described Kelce after the game.

Mahomes finished 23-of-37 for 249 yards, three touchdowns and a late-game interception. 92 yards went to Kelce.

"Travis always has the great nicknames," smiled Mahomes. "I just try to win, man. At the end of the day that's what I try to do. It's not like I'm planning these things where I'm throwing sidearm or whatever it is, spinning, running around. I always say, I'm a competitor, I'm going to find whatever way I can do to make our team have success. Today was a spin and a little, I don't know, a basketball shot that ended up a touchdown."

Ever the competitor, Brady would not go down without a fight, hitting wide receiver Mike Evans for a touchdown on the next drive to narrow the deficit to 21-10. Tampa Bay turned the Chiefs over on downs on the next possession, when Mahomes could not connect with Edwards-Helaire on a fourth-down try. But on the very next play, Brady was fooled by Chiefs cornerback L'Jarius Sneed, never seeing him as he streaked to the quarterback for a strip-sack.

The Chiefs defense held the Buccaneers to three rushing yards in the game, as their offense would score five touchdowns. Kicker Matthew Wright, signed that week as the Chiefs' latest Harrison Butker replacement, went 2-of-2 on field goals and made all five extra points.

After a disappointing day in Indianapolis, Kansas City's offensive line set the tone early, pushing the Buccaneers around and opening windows for Edwards-Helaire and rookie Isiah Pacheco to ground and pound for 155 combined rushing yards. All three tight ends — Kelce, Noah Gray, and Jody Fortson — scored touchdowns.

Brady threw more than 50 passes for 385 yards and three touchdowns, but Barrett's defense failed him. After he had giggled at the expense of the Chiefs, his Buccaneers allowed 41 points while only managing to score 31. Despite a two-score margin in a 41-31 final, Kansas City controlled the game from wire to wire.

A "coming-out party" indeed. ∎

Travis Kelce was a force in the win over the Bucs, catching nine passes for 92 yards and a touchdown.

Chiefs 30, Raiders 29

October 10, 2022 • Kansas City, Missouri

THE ARROWHEAD ADVANTAGE

Travis Kelce's Monster Day Caps Comeback Against Raiders

Eight nights after jumping out to a 21-3 lead over the Tampa Bay Buccaneers on *Sunday Night Football,* the Kansas City Chiefs were back in front of a national audience for *Monday Night Football* against their most bitter division rival: the Las Vegas Raiders.

This time, however, it was the Chiefs as the team trailing on their home field in the first half.

With points on three of their first four possessions, the Raiders led 17-0. Kansas City had punted twice, its offensive line giving up two sacks to standout defensive end Maxx Crosby. Kicker Matthew Wright, who had offered fans some relief in the special teams department after his perfect outing against Tampa Bay, had missed a 41-yarder.

The Chiefs badly needed a spark — one that would eventually come from two sources: running back Jerick McKinnon and the rabid fans of GEHA Field at Arrowhead Stadium.

Dealing with second-and-17 at the Kansas City 36-yard line after Crosby's second sack, quarterback Patrick Mahomes handed the ball to McKinnon. Initially touched by the Raiders after about two yards, McKinnon broke the tackles of three defenders before dashing up the left sideline for a gain of 30 and a first down.

Halfway through the second quarter, the Chiefs finally had life — and that feeling grew as Mahomes delivered a touchdown pass to tight end Travis Kelce a couple of plays later. The score awoke the Arrowhead crowd, something that eventually became a problem for referee Carl Cheffers.

With less than two minutes to go in the half on a third down at midfield, Raiders quarterback Derek Carr stepped up, not seeing that defensive lineman Chris Jones had overpowered Las Vegas right tackle Jermaine Eluemunor off the edge. Jones chased Carr from behind as the quarterback looked upfield, knocking the ball free with his right arm before landing on him for a strip-sack.

Jones had recovered the football, but Cheffers let his penalty flag fly, calling him for roughing-the-passer. Rather than the Chiefs regaining possession at the Las Vegas 42, the Raiders kept the ball and advanced to the Kansas City 40.

Head coach Andy Reid was uncharacteristically visibly irate with Cheffers, and the Kansas City crowd rained down with boos.

"I've seen him that angry but not about a call on the football field," joked Mahomes after the game. "If coach is pretty animated, he's a pretty even keeled guy so he must not have agreed with it."

Travis Kelce put on a show against the division rival Raiders with the unique combination of four touchdowns on seven catches for 25 yards.

The call obviously baffled Jones.

"I am 325 pounds, OK?" he said. "What do you want me to do? What do you want me to do? I'm running full speed trying to get the quarterback. I hit the ball, what do you want me to do?"

The Las Vegas drive ended with Raiders kicker Daniel Carlson booting a 50-yard field-goal attempt through the uprights, only to be bested by Wright, who made up for his early gaffe by setting a franchise record with a 59-yard field goal as the second quarter expired.

Even though the successful kick made history, the Arrowhead crowd persisted with loud boos as the teams — and referees — ran into the locker room for halftime. The fans sustained the energy through the 15-minute break in action.

Feeding off the Arrowhead faithful to begin the second half, Mahomes dialed up Kelce for touchdowns on two straight possessions, giving the Chiefs their first lead of the game, 24-20 late in the third quarter. Mahomes would hit Kelce for a fourth touchdown in the game's final frame to make it 30-23.

Reid described Kelce's stat line of 25 yards and a career-high four touchdowns as "a pretty good day, but a weird number," and Mahomes complimented the Raiders' plan for Kelce, comparing it to the style of physicality and attention previously seen from a Bill Belichick defense.

Predictably, Kelce did not want to discuss his personal showcase after the game.

"I'm not even thinking about it like that," said the tight end. "It was a fun game to see everybody rally together like that. Being down by 17, nobody cracked, you didn't see doubt in anybody's eyes. All it did was build the beast, made us rally together, circle the wagons in a way and fight for each other."

Wide receiver Marquez Valdes-Scantling, who led the Chiefs with 90 receiving yards, made sure to let reporters know the effort came on the night of his 28th birthday.

Las Vegas made it interesting late in the fourth quarter, with Carr finding All-Pro wide receiver Davante Adams deep down the middle of the field for a 48-yard touchdown, his second score of the game.

Now behind 30-29 and wanting a victory, Raiders head coach Josh McDaniels left the offense on the field for a two-point conversion try. McDaniels turned to running back Josh Jacobs, who finished with 154 rushing yards and an early touchdown.

On the game-deciding play, Jones met Jacobs at the goal line, preventing the two points, a defining moment in the eyes of Chiefs safety Justin Reid.

"In training camp, we made a statement that on the defensive side of the ball, we wanted to be an attitude defense," said the defensive back. "When the opportunity fell in our lap to finish that game on the defensive side, we wanted to do that. We didn't want to always have to rely on the offense." ∎

Jerick McKinnon only had eight carries in the win but made them count with 53 yards on the ground.

Bills 24, Chiefs 20

October 16, 2022 • Kansas City, Missouri

GONE IN 64 SECONDS

Patrick Mahomes Can't Find a Way Late in Loss to Bills

In a budding conference rivalry that had been defined by the "13 seconds" of the 2021 Divisional Round for nine months, the Kansas City Chiefs — and their grim reaper — had 64 ticks and two timeouts this time around.

A 14-yard touchdown pass from quarterback Josh Allen to tight end Dawson Knox saw the Buffalo Bills up 24-20 over the Chiefs with 1:04 to go in the game.

If quarterback Patrick Mahomes could get up the field the last time these two teams met at GEHA Field at Arrowhead Stadium, he would surely be able to find a way again, right?

Not on this day.

Beginning at their own 25-yard line, Mahomes rolled to his right. Throwing on the run, he narrowly missed wide receiver Mecole Hardman down the right sideline.

"If I can just barely maybe hit Mecole in that first one and get that chunk play, then it might be different," Mahomes said after the game.

The big play was not to be — but the officials did call a defensive holding call on Buffalo, resetting the down.

Now, at the 30-yard line with less than a minute to go, Mahomes dropped back. He glanced to his left, then to his right and fired a pass to rookie wide receiver Skyy Moore. Cornerback Taron Johnson stepped in front of Moore and intercepted the football.

"They were in a shell-type defense," explained Mahomes. "We had a corner route, and he had dropped back... You could see, I wanted to reset and throw it to him fast, and [Matt] Milano was in the way, and by the time I reset and threw it to him again, [Johnson] made a great play and got back in there.

"That's a good defense. That's a good player. You're at the end of the game, you're trying to press the issue and trying to get some completions because you've got to score a touchdown. But he made a good play when it counted."

Allen out-dueled Mahomes, throwing for 329 yards and three touchdowns, including tosses to Gabe Davis and Stephon Diggs, who capitalized on one-on-one matchups with rookie fourth-round cornerback Joshua Williams. Williams saw extended playing time for the first time in his young career due to the hamstring injuries of rookie first-rounder Trent McDuffie and veteran Rashad Fenton.

Diggs exploded for 148 receiving yards as running back Devin Singletary ran for 85 yards on the ground.

Mahomes had 338 yards, two touchdowns, and two interceptions. Mahomes' first pick happened on the 14th play of Kansas City's first drive of the game, as he tried to find wide receiver Marquez Valdes-Scantling in the end zone. Bills rookie Kaiir Elam came down with the 50-50 ball.

Mahomes' second interception ended the game.

"He was trying to make something happen and [Johnson] did a nice job of cutting it," said Chiefs head coach Andy Reid. "He was trying to make something happen. Normally he does. That one the guy made a nice play on it."

Kansas City took an early 7-3 lead in the second quarter when wide receiver JuJu Smith-Schuster scored

Patrick Mahomes threw for 338 yards and two touchdowns, but also added two interceptions in the loss to the Bills.

his first touchdown as a Chief. Smith-Schuster shook off three defenders with a nifty spin to run upfield for a 42-yard score as part of a team-high 113-yard day. Mahomes' second touchdown — to Hardman — tied the game at 17 in the third quarter.

Just one week after Matthew Wright set the field-goal record at 59, Harrison Butker — playing for the first time since Week 1 — broke it by converting a 62-yarder to tie the game at 10 as the first half expired. Butker missed a 51-yard field goal on the Chiefs' first possession of the second half with the game tied at 10 before his fourth-quarter 44-yard field goal gave the Chiefs a 20-17 lead.

Allen spoiled the kicker's return — making for a grim day in Kansas City. ∎

Chiefs 44, 49ers 23
October 23, 2022 • Santa Clara, California

HEEDING THE CALL ON THE WEST COAST

Chiefs Blast into Bye Week with Dominant Win Over Niners

The Kansas City Chiefs traveled to Santa Clara for their final game before their bye week, a late afternoon start against the San Francisco 49ers. Heading into the matchup, the Chiefs were still searching for some semblance of an identity.

Kansas City was 4-2 with two AFC West wins and a confidence-instilling outing against the Tampa Bay Buccaneers, but losses against the Indianapolis Colts and Buffalo Bills provided easy fodder to the skeptics.

Entering Week 7 against the Chiefs, the 49ers' defense was allowing an average of just 14.8 points to its opponent in 2022, as well as a league-low of 255.8 yards per game, not allowing more than 28 points or 308 yards to any opponent all season.

With a nod to the popular video game, *Call of Duty,* Kansas City erupted for six touchdowns and more than 529 net yards, defeating San Francisco 44-23 in a statement win ahead of their break.

"I had a free night on Friday [ahead of the game], so I told [JuJu Smith-Schuster], 'I'll get on [*Call of Duty*] with y'all for a little while,'" said Chiefs quarterback Patrick Mahomes, who threw for 423 yards, three touchdowns, and just one interception. "It was me, Travis [Kelce], Marquez [Valdes-Scantling], and JuJu.

Marquez and JuJu are really good. Me and Travis are just all right. We did our part and we went three for three with three wins in war zone, which I don't do often. So I felt pretty good about it going into the game."

The *Call of Duty* session translated to a productive day of modern warfare at Levi's Stadium. Smith-Schuster had seven receptions for 124 yards and a touchdown, Valdes-Scantling had three receptions for 111 yards and Kelce had six receptions for 98 yards.

"It's cool when you get away from the facility and you're doing kid-like things and you're on the headset, talking, joking around, and talking about the week," added Mahomes. "It gets your mind off of football. And it's about building those relationships. And so it's definitely cool to kind of see these guys, even if it's on the game, outside of the facility."

Both teams shook up their running back rooms ahead of the game, with the Chiefs opting to promote rookie seventh-rounder Isiah Pacheco to their starter. The 49ers acquired Christian McCaffrey from the Carolina Panthers in the days prior. Each back had eight carries, with Pacheco outpacing McCaffrey 43-38.

Though they eventually won, the Chiefs did not make it easy for themselves, with the 49ers scoring the first 10

Patrick Mahomes, Andy Reid, and the Chiefs bounced back in a big way following the loss to the Bills, taking it to the fellow contender, 44-23.

points. San Francisco kicker Robbie Gould nailed a 30-yard field goal on its first possession, followed by safety Talanoa Hufanga intercepting Mahomes.

Working with a short field, 49ers quarterback Jimmy Garoppolo orchestrated an efficient, four-play drive, concluding with an 8-yard pass to wide receiver Ray-Ray McCloud in the end zone.

But San Francisco's lead would evaporate as quickly as wide receiver Mecole Hardman can dash down a football field. An 8-yard pop-pass in the first quarter and a 25-yard sweep in the second quarter saw Hardman in the end zone twice. He later added another touchdown in the fourth quarter on a 3-yard sweep, becoming the first wide receiver in the Super Bowl era with two or more rushing touchdowns and one or more receiving touchdowns in a single game.

"I think I have a good feel for it," said Hardman of those sweep-type plays. "Honestly, just the vision and trying to find the little holes and the little gas between the defenses you try to hit. If you can get through them with speed and you try to get somebody one on one, it's going to be a long day for that defender. So I'm just trying to do that."

The Chiefs were winning 14-13 late in the second quarter when Skyy Moore muffed his second punt of the season, setting up Garoppolo at the Kansas City 12. But unlike in Indianapolis, the Chiefs' defense held strong, and on third down, the quarterback carelessly floated a ball up in the end zone, right into the hands of rookie cornerback Jaylen Watson.

Moore breathed a sigh of relief.

"I know he wants that play back — he came over and said, 'Thank you,'" said Watson. "That's Skyy. I am glad we got the opportunity to stop them from putting points on the board. That was just a big turning point of the game."

The Chiefs maintained the lead, but San Francisco continued to hang around into the fourth quarter, when a 15-yard touchdown by tight end George Kittle cut it to 28-23. But that would be the last time the 49ers would score.

Linebacker Willie Gay Jr. returned to the lineup after serving his four-game suspension, collecting eight tackles and splitting a sack with cornerback L'Jarius Sneed. The Chiefs sacked Garoppolo a total of five times, and safety Juan Thornhill intercepted backup Brock Purdy, who had replaced Garoppolo.

The Chiefs closed the game on a 16-0 run, featuring the third touchdown by Hardman, a safety from defensive end Frank Clark going up against left tackle Trent Williams, and then a long Smith-Schuster score to seal it.

"I saw a relentless football," said Chiefs head coach Andy Reid. "Nothing tells you that more than what Frank did at the end there with the safety against one of the greats (Williams), who will go down as one of the great offensive linemen that ever played this game."

Kansas City entered its bye week with five wins in seven contests.

"We lost a couple of games that we wanted to win," admitted Mahomes. "But when you look back on it and you're 5-2 and you're first in the AFC West, you can't ask to be in a better position.

"Now we have to recalibrate, get off our feet, get our bodies back, and then learn. Because when we come back in this next best stretch, we're gonna be ready to go and try to make a push to get to the playoffs and then try to get to the Super Bowl." ■

The Kansas City defense made life hard on the 49ers, forcing three turnovers and sacking San Francisco five times.

THE WINDS OF TRADE

Key Midseason Trades Help the Chiefs in the Short Term and Long Run

Kansas City Chiefs general manager Brett Veach is never conservative when it comes to making the roster better at any point in the calendar year, and he proved it once again as he made two trades during the 2022 NFL season.

October 27, 2022: The Chiefs trade for wide receiver Kadarius Toney

In late October, the Chiefs sent their third-round compensatory pick as well as a sixth-round pick to the New York Giants in exchange for wide receiver Kadarius Toney, someone that Veach apparently had his eye on for a long time.

"It was something that he actually approached me about during the offseason," said quarterback Patrick Mahomes after the trade. "He's kept me in the loop on everything. It didn't work then, so you get locked in during the season and focused on the guys that are in the building and how can we have success with these guys. We've had a lot of success, so he came after me after, I think, the (Week 7) San Fran game and came back and said this might happen during the bye, we're talking with him and everything like that. Luckily enough for us, it did happen, and we were able to get another talented playmaker in that receiving room."

Toney entered the league as the No. 20 overall pick made by the Giants during the first round of the 2021 NFL Draft. Appearing in only 10 games during his rookie season (due to placement on the COVID-19 list and injuries), the 6-foot, 193-pound receiver caught 39 passes for 420 yards. A hamstring issue had limited him to just two games in 2022. He had made just two receptions.

The addition of Toney immediately helped the Chiefs, who needed a punt returner as rookie Skyy Moore struggled at the position. He scored his first career touchdown in his second game as a Chief in Week 10 against the Jacksonville Jaguars. Between the Giants and Chiefs, Toney finished the season with 14 catches for 171 yards and two touchdowns. He made five catches for 36 yards in the Chiefs' Divisional Round win over the Jacksonville Jaguars.

Toney was hampered by a midseason hamstring injury that cost him three games, but when he was healthy and able to play, he flashed the traits that made him a first-round pick in New York. That could be important for Kansas City in the future, as they have Toney on his rookie contract.

Wide receiver Kadarius Toney was acquired from the New York Giants in October.

November 1, 2022: Chiefs trade Rashad Fenton to Falcons, activate Trent McDuffie

In the final hour of the NFL trade deadline, the Chiefs sent cornerback Rashad Fenton to the Atlanta Falcons in exchange for a conditional seventh-round pick.

Fenton, 25, had been drafted by Kansas City during the sixth round of the 2019 NFL Draft. He appeared in 47 games (16 starts), accumulating 20 passes defensed, two interceptions and 123 tackles (95 solo). Sending Fenton to the Falcons provided the Chiefs with $1.4 million in additional 2022 cap space, and they used the free roster spot to activate Trent McDuffie, who had been on injured reserve stemming from a Week 1 hamstring injury.

The midseason move was more of a statement by the Chiefs than anything else. They believed in their rookies — and especially the "Fab Five."

The trade acknowledged Kansas City had seen enough from its rookies to feel comfortable moving forward.

Seventh-rounder Jaylen Watson entered the lineup when McDuffie went down, showcasing his abilities when he returned an interception 99 yards leading to a Week 2 win over the Los Angeles Chargers.

When Fenton missed two games due to a hamstring injury — as McDuffie was not *quite* ready yet — the Chiefs had to turn to rookie fourth-rounder Joshua Williams, who showed he could serve the team as ample depth in the case of another injury.

The underlying key to the deal, however, might have very well been rookie seventh-rounder Nazeeh Johnson, the little-known member of the "Fab Five" who the Chiefs added to their active roster in late September. Clearing McDuffie's spot while keeping Fenton would have meant the Chiefs risking Johnson through waivers. There is a good chance he would have been claimed.

Seeing the writing on the wall, the Chiefs traded Fenton to the Falcons, created a little cap room and keeping the four cornerbacks they drafted in 2022. ■

Head coach Andy Reid talks with cornerback Trent McDuffie during a January 2023 game against the Raiders. Despite a hamstring injury, the rookie cornerback saw action in 11 regular season games.

Chiefs 20, Titans 17 (OT)
November 6, 2022 • Kansas City, Missouri

'MR. NOVEMBER'

Patrick Mahomes and Chiefs Continue November Run in Win Over Titans

Both good and bad news met the Kansas City Chiefs as they came out of their Week 8 bye. First, the good.

After missing six games due to a Week 1 hamstring injury, rookie first-round cornerback Trent McDuffie was activated off injured reserve. To make room for McDuffie, the Chiefs surprised many when they shipped veteran cornerback Rashad Fenton to the Atlanta Falcons at the trade deadline. The move signified general manager Brett Veach doubling down on McDuffie and his four fellow rookie defensive backs.

As McDuffie returned to the youthful defense, a new face arrived on offense: wide receiver Kadarius Toney, who the New York Giants sent to Kansas City in exchange for a pair of 2023 draft picks.

In addition to that, the calendar had turned to November — the month in which quarterback Patrick Mahomes plays his best football. The last time Mahomes had lost in the year's 11th month was November 10, 2019, to none other than their upcoming opponent, the Tennessee Titans.

But as mentioned, there was also some bad.

After his best game of the season against the San Francisco 49ers, defensive end Frank Clark began serving a two-game suspension. A solace there is though the Chiefs would miss Clark, they finally could count on a healthy Mike Danna, who had been nursing a calf injury since Week 2.

And speaking of injuries, the Titans arrived to GEHA Field at Arrowhead Stadium with a crucial one. Quarterback Ryan Tannehill, who had missed Tennessee's previous game against the Houston Texans due to an ankle injury, needed to sit another week.

That meant a *Sunday Night Football* matchup of Mahomes, a former MVP and Super Bowl MVP, against Malik Willis, a rookie about to start his second career game.

Given the injury to their quarterback, the Titans predictably devised a game plan heavily featuring Derrick Henry, the All-Pro running back known for picking up chunks of tough yardage even when defenders know he is about to get the ball. Willis completed five passes all game.

Henry shined against Kansas City, rushing nine times for 92 yards in the first half, including single rushes of 24 and 56 yards, which led to back-to-back second-quarter touchdowns and a 14-9 Tennessee lead as the teams headed into the locker room. The Chiefs' front seven went to their quarters frustrated.

"We just kind of knocking the rust off of the bye week," explained linebacker Nick Bolton. "We kind of start off a little sloppy tackling wise. Couple bad fits here and there and kind of led to explosive runs."

Kansas City understood that allowing Henry to continue having his way in the second half would not lead to a victory.

Patrick Mahomes lit up the Titans through the air, completing 43 passes for 446 yards and a touchdown.

"We came at halftime and was like, 'If we stop that,' — which, as you can see when you do, that it kind of limits it," added defensive tackle Khalen Saunders. "So I was happy coming out [the] half to get them stops."

In the second half, the Chiefs defense allowed Henry only 23 yards and the Titans three points, buying time for Mahomes and the offense to wake up after managing only one first-half touchdown to wide receiver Mecole Hardman followed by seven straight empty possessions over three quarters.

Midway through the fourth, as Kansas City trailed 17-9, the home crowd was silent.

The Titans' front — led by defensive tackle Jeffery Simmons, who had called his shot leading into the game — had indeed "dominated" the Chiefs' line, without Titans head coach Mike Vrabel needing to blitz. Kansas City could not manage any kind of push in the running game — and Mahomes was hardly comfortable.

As it usually goes in November, it all changed quickly.

Facing third-and-17 with half a quarter to play and the game in the balance, Mahomes scrambled 20 yards for the first down. Kansas City's offense stayed alive, leading to a moment reminiscent of the 2019 AFC Championship game. Working in the red zone, Mahomes scrambled to his right, running 14 yards for a touchdown to bring the Chiefs within two at 17-15.

A couple of defensive holding flags later, he scrambled to the other side, sneaking just to the right of the pylon to tie the game.

In overtime, Mahomes leaned on a familiar tight end, Travis Kelce, who led the Chiefs with 106 yards, and a less familiar one, Noah Gray, who went up to make a crucial third-and-1, 27-yard catch that required a high-point above Titans cornerback Roger McCreary.

"I want to give [Gray] more and more chances because I think he can be a big part of this offense," said Mahomes. "That whole tight end room has been great for us this season. But for him to make that catch in that moment, that was a tough catch that he made, that was a big one for us."

Mahomes would add that Gray's catch was probably the reason the Chiefs won, as it set up kicker Harrison Butker to redeem himself for earlier extra-point and field-goal misses. Butker was good from 28 yards, and the defense forced Willis to four-and-out to clinch the game.

A week after his induction into the Texas Tech Hall of Fame, "Mr. November" began his favorite month with a collegiate stat line: 43-of-68 for 446 yards, one passing touchdown, 63 rushing yards, one rushing touchdown and the lone pick off a deflection. ∎

Tight end Noah Gray had three catches for 45 yards in the overtime win over the Titans.

Chiefs 27, Jaguars 17

November 13, 2022 • Kansas City, Missouri

AN UNASSUMING PLAYOFF PREVIEW

Chiefs Take Care of Jags in a Sign of Things to Come

The Jacksonville Jaguars arrived to GEHA Field at Arrowhead Stadium with a 3-6 record — with Kansas City being the team's final stop before a Week 11 bye week.

Nobody at the time expected the midseason tilt between the Jaguars and Chiefs to be an AFC playoff preview — and why would they? Former Chiefs offensive coordinator Doug Pederson and quarterback Trevor Lawrence had been struggling to muster any sort of momentum, and the Jacksonville franchise appeared poised for another top-10 selection in the NFL Draft.

The Jaguars were unassuming, making the environment ripe for a surprise onside kick to begin the game. But while Jacksonville recovered, the Kansas City defense forced a punt on the opening drive.

"They came in the game [and] they knew that they had to steal a play," said Chiefs safety Justin Reid. "They definitely came in and they caught us off guard with that one. For the defense to come out and get a stop, I think that was major for the momentum of the game — to keep control of it and not let it get out of hand early to where it started to turn into chaos to where we were scrambling."

In only his second game as a Chief, wide receiver Kadarius Toney opened the game's scoring, though quarterback Patrick Mahomes never expected him to be a target on a play that would turn into his first career touchdown.

At the Jacksonville 6, Mahomes faked a pop pass to Toney, who leaked out to the right flat. Mahomes eventually looked his way, and though wide open, he caught the ball so close to the right sideline, he had to tip-toe in the end zone for the score.

"It was funny because we had some plays designed for him to score but if you would've told me one play that I didn't think he was going to score on it was that one, but it was cool to see," said Mahomes. "Everybody was excited for him. Luckily, he didn't run out of bounds, he was getting close there on the sideline. I actually heard him as the route was going on, going, 'Ayyyyyy' because he was wide open so that helped me out a little bit."

As Toney caught his first career touchdown in the first quarter, wide receiver Marquez Valdes-Scantling brought in his first touchdown as a Chief early in the second to give Kansas City a 14-0 lead. Valdes-Scantling felt 10 weeks to be enough to wait to get in the end zone.

"It's been a minute," said Valdes-Scantling. "It's been a minute and we were able to draw something up for me and get me one. JuJu [Smith☐Schuster] did a great job of attracting his corner now and [Justin Watson] clearing it out — it kind of left me one on one to

The Chiefs kept the pressure on Jacksonville quarterback Trevor Lawrence all day with five sacks.

find a spot on the other side of the field and Pat gave me a nice, easy one."

Smith-Schuster would leave the game on the next drive after suffering a concussion at the hands of Jaguars safety Andre Cisco. After initially throwing a flag on the play, the referees picked it up, later citing shoulder-to-shoulder contact. That did not make much sense to Chiefs head coach Andy Reid, as Smith-Schuster laid on the ground as he received medical attention to his head and neck.

"It's not good," said Reid. "That's not a good feeling at all. And that's what I tried to explain to the officials — that guys don't get hit in the shoulder and lay around like that right there. There's more to it — somewhere, the head was involved. And so, that's what the rules were put in for — for that type of thing."

In Smith-Schuster's absence, tight ends Noah Gray and Travis Kelce added touchdowns, and rookie Isiah Pacheco recovered from an early fumble to run 16 times for 82 yards. Reid went right back to Pacheco after the fumble, allowing him to run "angrier," as he described.

"That just allows me to know that my teammates and coaches have my back, and they trust me," said Pacheco.

Jaguars wide receiver Christian Kirk posted 105 yards and two touchdowns, but the Chiefs defense held dynamic running back Travis Etienne to 45 yards to control the game and pick up the 27-17 victory.

Kansas City continued to get defensive production at every level, beginning up front with defensive tackle Chris Jones, who led the team with 1.5 sacks on the day. Jones wasn't alone, with the team finishing with a total of 5.0 sacks. Jones' split of a sack with veteran Carlos Dunlap gave Dunlap 100 for his career.

"Playing 10-plus years, getting a 100-plus sacks to be in that elite category of the guys who have ever done it," said Dunlap, "so [to] get that done today and to share it with a guy who has potential to be up there as well was a very special moment."

The Jaguars left Arrowhead looking like a team entering its bye with years of development ahead of them if they were to make the postseason.

Pederson, an old friend, used his break to find the express lane. ∎

Isiah Pacheco had a strong day running the ball with 16 carries for 82 yards.

Chiefs 30, Chargers 27
November 20, 2022 • Inglewood, California

ENCORE

Travis Kelce and Chiefs Pull Out Yet Another Thriller Against Chargers

When two in-division teams — such as the Kansas City Chiefs and Los Angeles Chargers — settle their previous three matchups by a one-score margin, as they feature two of the game's brightest young stars in Patrick Mahomes and Justin Herbert, the NFL is basically left without an option.

That game must be played in prime time. And so, it was decided.

Following last year's overtime thriller in Los Angeles and the Chiefs and Chargers' Week 2 Thursday Night Football matchup that saw Kansas City win 27-24, the league flexed 2022's second edition into *Sunday Night Football*. The original matchup, an AFC North battle between the Cincinnati Bengals and Pittsburgh Steelers, was moved to the late-afternoon time slot.

Seven lead changes under the lights of SoFi Stadium later, the league would learn it undoubtedly made the right decision. The last time the Chiefs met in Los Angeles, tight end Travis Kelce would famously "call game" with a 34-yard overtime touchdown.

History just about repeated itself in 2022.

Behind 27-23 with less than a minute to go, Mahomes had the Kansas City offense inside the Los Angeles red zone.

There are few teams in the league that offer a player that can handle Kelce one on one, and the Chargers are one of them, with former 2018 first-round safety Derwin James. But Kelce had his way with James on this occasion; before the final drive, the tight end already had two touchdowns.

And they were once again with the game hanging in the balance. Lined up to Mahomes' right, Kelce ran a slant across the middle of the field, and James was hindered by wide receiver Justin Watson his way with a tailing defender.

Mahomes delivered the ball to Kelce with a yard of space, and a diving James could not reach him. He took it 17 yards for his third touchdown of the night. Kelce spiked the ball into the divider as what was a generous number of Chiefs fans in attendance went wild.

"If he's man to man, I'm going to give him a chance, and he's going win most of them," Mahomes — who finished 20-of-34 for 329 yards and the three scores — said of Kelce. "Obviously, they got Derwin, so Derwin's going to win his battles because he's probably the best safety in the league. But yeah, I'm going to give my guy a chance because I know how special he is."

Kelce being so productive as he slowly approaches his mid-30s is no coincidence.

"I'm an older dog," Kelce said after the game. "Throughout my years, I just learned from situations that I've been through on the football field — situations that I've seen on the football field. I just keep accumulating all that data and just put it in this computer up here (pointing at his head) and hope that I can use it to my advantage."

Travis Kelce once again dominated the Chargers, this time catching six passes for 115 yards and three touchdowns, including the winning score.

Kansas City left 31 seconds on the clock, providing Herbert and the Chargers, who had all three timeouts, one final opportunity down 30-27. Defensive tackle Chris Jones sacked Herbert for a loss of 5 yards on first down, leading to second-and-15.

Pressured by defensive end Frank Clark, Herbert lofted a ball off his back foot, attempting to wide receiver Keenan Allen, who had returned to the team after a two-game absence. Defensive backs L'Jarius Sneed and Deon Bush met at the ball, deflecting it in the air. Linebacker Nick Bolton came down with the interception to end the game.

As has become routine with the Chargers, they entered the division matchup with a lengthy injury list, including tight end Gerald Everett, left tackle Rashawn Slater and pass rusher Joey Bosa. Wide receiver Mike Williams left the game in the first quarter due to an ankle injury.

In their absences, other Chargers stepped up, with second-year receiver Joshua Palmer leading the way for eight catches and 106 yards. Allen was next with 94 yards and running back Austin Ekeler had 83 rushing yards and a touchdown.

As Clyde Edwards-Helaire suffered a high-ankle sprain, rookie running back Isiah Pacheco broke out for 107 yards on 15 carries. Missing wide receiver JuJu Smith-Schuster, out with a concussion, veteran wide receiver Justin Watson had three catches for 67 yards. Rookie wideout Skyy Moore made five catches for 63 yards, keeping his head in the game after being replaced by Kadarius Toney on punt return.

"It's great," said head coach Andy Reid. "He had punt returns that were a bit of a mess, but he had never done that. The guys kept encouraging him through this, whether it was his (wide receivers) coach, Joe [Bleymaier] or (offensive quality control coach) Connor [Embree]. They just keep encouraging him. The players stuck by him."

No Chiefs pointed fingers in Los Angeles, even as the Chargers stole back the lead three times. On this night, the fourth time was a charm. ∎

While the Chiefs gave up 27 points to Austin Ekeler and the Chargers, they limited Los Angeles to only seven points in the second half as Kansas City rallied for the win.

Chiefs 26, Rams 10

November 27, 2022 • Kansas City, Missouri

CHAMPS TURNED CHUMPS

Defending Champ Rams No Match for Chiefs

There are times every year when anticipation and excitement in May — the month in which the NFL releases the upcoming schedule — simply does not translate to the matchup that plays out six months later.

There may have been no better example of this in 2022 than the reigning Super Bowl champion Los Angeles Rams visiting the Kansas City Chiefs in Week 12. As boastful hosts of four consecutive AFC Championship games, Chiefs fans in the summer saw this matchup in the distant future as a proper measuring stick — a late-season game to determine just how close Kansas City was to returning to Super Bowl glory.

But the Rams fell off the map — so far off that at 3-7, they shut down starting quarterback Matt Stafford due to a head and neck injury. With backup Jon Wolford facing the same, Rams head coach Sean McVay turned the keys to third-year undrafted free agent Bryce Perkins for the first start of his career at GEHA Field at Arrowhead Stadium.

As to be expected, that plan did not go swimmingly for Los Angeles. Perkins finished 13-of-23 for 100 yards, one touchdown and two fourth-quarter interceptions, with the Chiefs defense allowing its lowest point total of the season.

The Chiefs' defensive play provided relief for the offense, which scored a touchdown just once in six red-zone trips.

"We got to do a little better in the red zone," said head coach Andy Reid after the game. "That's a place we're normally pretty good, but we were off just a tick tonight and we'll go back to the drawing board on that and make sure we take care of that."

Kansas City's defense forced a three-and-out on Rams' first possession, and punter Riley Dixon came on to punt. Inside the Rams' 10, Dixon drove it to midfield, where Skyy Moore muffed the football for the third time this season.

The Rams recovered, marking Moore's final punt return... until the AFC Championship game (but more on that later).

At this stage of this particular season, Moore needed a break, and with Kadarius Toney injured, special teams coordinator Dave Toub called on Justin Watson as the next man up. The fans at Arrowhead sarcastically cheered as Watson successfully corralled the ball on the next punt opportunity.

Reid likes to go right back to players when they make mistakes, and though the Chiefs had to bench Moore on special teams, they did so on offense. Quarterback Patrick Mahomes led Moore down the left sideline on an 18-yard pass that required him to fully extend his arms to bring it in.

"[Moore] came back and had that nice catch right after that," said Reid, "which for a young kid kind of get that out of his mind I thought was a plus."

The Chiefs completed the drive when Mahomes hit tight end Travis Kelce, who juked cornerback Jalen

Guard Nick Allegretti (73) and the offensive line limited superstar defensive tackle Aaron Donald to only three tackles and no sacks.

Ramsey out of his shoes, compiling about 20 yards after the catch for a 34-yard touchdown to give Kansas City a 7-0 lead. Kelce led the Chiefs with a modest 57 receiving yards on the day.

"[Kelce] was my primary read and some of those plays when he's in man coverage you just let him work," said Mahomes. "I didn't know what he was going to do honestly because he had a deep crosser but those are some of those routes sometimes that he just breaks out, so I was just kind of hanging on there. I know he made a good move, got him the ball. [It was a] little behind him but he ended up making a good run at the catch and then scoring a touchdown."

Mahomes, who was 27-of-42 for 320 yards, knocked on the door the rest of the afternoon but never scored again, later throwing an interception in the end zone.

Mahomes' pick came as the Rams only trailed the Chiefs 20-10 in the fourth quarter, but Kansas City cornerback L'Jarius Sneed gave the football right back to Mahomes with a takeaway of his own two plays later.

Linebacker Nick Bolton sealed the win for Kansas City by intercepting the opposition for the second straight game on the next drive. Early in 2022, turnovers had been difficult to come by for the Chiefs defense, but that was two weeks in a row they forced the opposition into two.

"I kind of feel like our D-line did a hell of a job again today generating pressure and getting their hands up," said Bolton. "Shout out to [Carlos Dunlap] on that pick that was basically 75% him, 25% me – I give him credit on that one. But also, we're just catching the balls that come to us.

"We had a couple early in the year that we just dropped, so we just kind of made a focus on that and just get the ones they give us. Execute down the stretch and try to get our hands on as many footballs as we can."

Running back Isiah Pacheco rushed for 69 yards and a touchdown on 22 carries, and kicker Harrison Butker made all four of his field-goal opportunities and both extra points.

The win clinched at least a five-game winning streak — or, in other words, the "Andy Reid special." The Chiefs have recorded a five-game win streak in all 10 seasons Reid has served the club as its head coach. ∎

THE KANSAS CITY CHIEFS' 2022 CHAMPIONSHIP SEASON

Bengals 27, Chiefs 24
December 4, 2022 • Cincinnati, Ohio

CLOSE, BUT NO CIGAR

Losing Streak Reaches Three Against Surging Bengals

Quarterback Patrick Mahomes had his Kansas City Chiefs on the verge of overcoming the only Achilles heel of his young, record-shattering career.

Coming off back-to-back touchdown drives, the Chiefs led the Cincinnati Bengals 24-20 early in the fourth quarter. On second-and-8, Mahomes fired a pass into the gut of tight end Travis Kelce just beyond the first-down marker.

Kelce turned upfield, gaining about 10 yards after the catch before he was quickly surrounded by three Bengals defenders. Cincinnati linebacker Germaine Pratt tugged and ripped at the ball.

Then the unthinkable happened: it shook loose.

"We knew that we needed to make a turnover," said Pratt. "Kelce sat down in a little weak spot of the defense. I just had an opportunity to go for the ball."

Pratt snagged it out of the air, giving Bengals quarterback Joe Burrow the ball back at the Cincinnati 47-yard line. Using a combination of short passes and runs, Burrow and the Bengals bled five minutes off the clock before running back Chris Evans scored the go-ahead 8-yard touchdown reception.

Cincinnati had pulled off what may have been a 14-point swing for a 27-24 lead.

Down three, Mahomes worked the Chiefs offense back into field-goal range at the Bengals' 33-yard line. But on third-and-3, Cincinnati defensive end Joseph Ossai beat Kansas City left tackle Orlando Brown Jr., getting to Mahomes for a 4-yard sack in a second effort.

After two perfect kicking weeks following his injury, kicker Harrison Butker came on for a 55-yard field goal. Lining up from the left hash, he sliced it wide right.

"[It's] very similar to what we've done before," said head coach Andy Reid after the game. "That's within [Butker's] range. You [need to] get that combination of the snap a little higher, and the kick a little stronger. You have to get that going, but it didn't happen."

Cincinnati built a 14-3 second-quarter lead by scoring touchdowns on the first two drives. Following the Bengals' second touchdown, a 12-yard pass from Burrow to wide receiver Tee Higgins, wide receiver Ja'Marr Chase got in the face of safety Justin Reid, drawing a taunting penalty.

Earlier in the week, the safety told Kansas City media members he would lock down Cincinnati tight end Hayden Hurst before amplifying his message using his official Twitter account, writing he promised to "lock everybody up."

Chase took exception, answering via his own Twitter account before posting 97 yards in the matchup. With starting running back Joe Mixon in concussion protocol, backup Samaje Perine ran all over the Chiefs for 106 yards. Burrow continued to remain frustratingly protected, as only Kansas City rookie George Karlaftis could manage a sack.

Patrick Mahomes and the Chiefs were stymied by the Bengals again, losing for the third consecutive time in the match up.

Kansas City battled back after the early deficit, with running back Jerick McKinnon scoring a touchdown in the second quarter. Defensive end Carlos Dunlap stopped the team that drafted him in 2010 on a fourth-down, goal-line try before the half, reminiscent of last year's AFC Championship game — in reverse.

The Chiefs took the lead early in the third quarter, 17-14, when running back Isiah Pacheco ran it in from 8 yards out. A Bengals field goal on the next drive tied the game at 17.

Kansas City fans were ready to pin up posters after Mahomes' Air Jordan-like jump-and-stretch over the goal line put the Chiefs ahead 24-17 late in the third quarter, but Kelce's crucial mistake would halt the printers.

The Bengals had indeed beaten Kansas City for a third consecutive time.

"I'm sure we're going to see those guys again come January," said Justin Reid. ∎

Above: Linebacker Willie Gay Jr. tries to chase down the elusive Joe Burrow. Burrow was effective scrambling, rushing for 46 yards and a touchdown. Opposite: Jerick McKinnon and the rushing attack for the Chiefs were effective with 138 yards and two touchdowns, but it wasn't enough to prevail over the rival Bengals.

Chiefs 34, Broncos 28
December 11, 2022 • Denver, Colorado

AVOIDING DISASTER IN DENVER

Chiefs Survive Furious Comeback by Broncos

In a peculiar way, Kansas City Chiefs fans were delighted when — weeks ahead of what was supposed to be a primetime matchup against their AFC West rival — the league decided to flex the club's matchup with the hated Denver Broncos out of *Sunday Night Football*.

Chiefs quarterback Patrick Mahomes is the NFL's greatest draw. If the league opted to flex out Kansas City, the Broncos would have to be having one of the worst seasons imaginable.

And really, they were. Denver entered the game with a 3-9 record and on a four-game losing streak — and the decision to trade for former Seattle Seahawks quarterback Russell Wilson had utterly failed.

The league likely expected the Chiefs to blow the doors off the Broncos on their home field. And to its credit, they were — until they suddenly weren't.

Kansas City began on a roll, scoring the game's first 27 points. Following two Harrison Butker field goals, Mahomes rolled out to his right, high stepping near the sideline to avoid diving Broncos nose tackle D.J. Jones. Mahomes flipped it sidearm to McKinnon, who took it 56 yards up the field for the score.

"That is just Pat being Pat," said McKinnon, who would score the next touchdown and lead the Chiefs with 112 receiving yards. "He is incredible at making plays like that. When he moves out of the pocket, he does a great job of keeping his eyes downfield. Once I saw he was out of the pocket, I kind of just tried to get downfield and he made an incredible play to get it down there. There were some great blocks down the field, and I was able to make a play."

Behind 20 in the second quarter, Denver head coach Nathaniel Hackett kept the offense on the field for a fourth-down try at midfield. Wilson faked a toss, attempting to fool the defense. Looking for a receiver short and to his right, Wilson lofted a pass intended for the stick, but Kansas City linebacker Willie Gay Jr. plucked it out of the air.

Gay stiff-armed Wilson, running it all the way back for a 47-yard touchdown.

Strangely enough, somehow, *that* is when the game became interesting.

Up 27-0 with less than three minutes to go in the first half, Mahomes threw an interception into the hands of linebacker Josey Jewell. Beginning in Kansas City territory, Wilson got the Broncos on the board as wide receiver Jerry Jeudy beat cornerback Joshua Williams for an 18-yard touchdown.

Denver cornerback Patrick Surtain picked Mahomes off on the next drive, and Wilson used his legs to get the Broncos within striking distance. Beating the clock, Wilson found Jeudy again right before halftime. 27-0 had turned to 27-14 in the blink of an eye.

Patrick Mahomes had an eventful day against the Broncos, throwing for 352 yards and three touchdowns, but also giving up three interceptions.

Denver kept the ball to begin the second half, with Hackett calling a screen for running back Marlon Mack at precisely the right time. Chiefs defensive coordinator Steve Spagnuolo had called a blitz, and Mack went the distance for a 66-yard touchdown.

The Broncos and Chiefs exchanged possessions before Mahomes finally stopped the bleeding. Pressured in the pocket on third-and-goal from the Denver 4, Mahomes evaded tacklers to extend the play, somehow connecting with wide receiver JuJu Smith-Schuster in the end zone, curbing the 21-0 run and giving the Chiefs a 34-21 lead.

"Putting points on the board helped us out a lot," said Smith-Schuster, who finished with nine catches for 74 yards. "It takes the cushion off of us and our defense but they're a great team and in divisional play, I've noticed that it's a dogfight no matter what their record is, they're going to come out and play their hearts out."

The Broncos continued to do just that, even after Wilson had to leave the game due to a concussion, as backup Brett Rypien hit Jeudy for his third touchdown of the game.

Once again nursing a one-score lead, at 34-28, Mahomes threw a third interception — and the second into the hands of Jewell. But a Chiefs defense that hit the opposing team's quarterback 11 times, including five sacks, would not be denied.

The game on the line, Kansas City defensive tackle Chris Jones hit Rypien as he threw, and the resulting rainbow pass fell perfectly into the hands of cornerback L'Jarius Sneed.

The Chiefs escaped what Mahomes would describe as "three bad decisions" in an otherwise-good stat line that included over 350 yards and three touchdowns.

"Luckily for me, the rest of the team stepped up," said Mahomes. "The defense made a lot of stops in critical moments. We were putting them in bad situations. Even the special teams was making field goals and (punter) Tommy [Townsend] flipped the field a couple of times for us. The guys around me stepped up and made some plays." ∎

JuJu Smith-Schuster had a strong game in the win over Denver, catching nine passes for 74 yards and a touchdown.

Chiefs 30, Texans 24 (OT)
December 18, 2022 • Houston, Texas

HOLDING ON FOR THE HOMECOMING

Patrick Mahomes Comes Home, Narrowly Avoids a Stunner

Entering Week 15, the Kansas City Chiefs simply needed to win to clinch their seventh straight AFC West title. Aside from the Chiefs being on the road, the circumstances could not have set up better.

Competing as a pro for the first time in his home state of Texas, quarterback Patrick Mahomes had drawn the Houston Texans.

At 1-11-1, the Texans were the worst team in football. In addition, top wideouts Brandin Cooks and Nico Collins could not play due to injury, and neither could standout rookie running back Dameon Pierce or cornerback Steven Nelson. The Houston coaching staff had decided it best to use a two-quarterback system… in the NFL.

It should have been comfortable for Kansas City; it took overtime.

The essence of an upset was in the air as the Texans, tied 24-24 with the Chiefs, forced a punt to begin the extra session. That meant a Houston field goal would end the game.

But after four quarters of playing inspired, competitive football, the Texans came crashing down back to Earth on offensive play number one.

Chasing Houston quarterback Davis Mills from behind, Chiefs defensive end Frank Clark wound up his right arm, clubbing the quarterback. The ball bounced up off the turf at NRG Stadium, and nearly 10 players pounced on it. Officials gathered to separate the pile, and as they did, Kansas City linebacker Willie Gay Jr. emerged with the football.

At Houston's 26, Mahomes handed the ball off to running back Jerick McKinnon, who juked left. Four blocks later, McKinnon trotted into the end zone untouched — and the Chiefs were AFC West champions.

Speaking to the media following the game, McKinnon said that Mahomes told him, "Two hands on the ball. Let's go."

McKinnon told Mahomes he was going to score.

"JuJu [Smith-Schuster] looked at me," started McKinnon. "He said, 'I got your block, bro. Find me when you get out there.' It worked out exactly like that. I made it to the second level, and I literally ran off of JuJu's block and was able to score. It's just crazy it worked out like that, man. It's crazy."

McKinnon also recorded the Chiefs' first touchdown, a 20-yard reception that opened up thanks to pre-snap

Andy Reid and the Chiefs narrowly escaped Houston with a win, prevailing 30-24 in overtime in a more competitive game than anticipated.

movement by returning wide receiver Kadarius Toney, who had missed the previous three games due to a hamstring injury. McKinnon's first touchdown tied the game 7-7 in the second quarter.

An Isiah Pacheco fumble at the Chiefs' 22 set the Texans up nicely, and Mills scrambled for a 17-yard touchdown two plays later. Kansas City scored on the next possession when Mahomes gunned a pass to Marquez Valdes-Scantling from four yards out.

Valdes-Scantling made a tough diving catch, but kicker Harrison Butker missed the extra point, allowing Houston to take a 14-13 lead into halftime. Butker would later miss a 51-yarder in the closing seconds of the fourth quarter that may have prevented overtime.

"Being a kicker is little like being a batter, and sometimes you get in a slump," said Chiefs head coach Andy Reid of Butker. "He's a great one, and he'll get through it, and then he'll come out of it even better than what he was. You got to keep kicking, and that's what we're going to do with him."

Mills and Mahomes continued to exchange blows in the second half, and a 5-yard scramble by the Kansas City quarterback — coupled with a two-point conversion — gave the Chiefs a three-point lead in the fourth quarter. More reliable than Butker on the day, Houston kicker Ka'imi Fairbairn nailed a 29-yarder in the fourth quarter to send it to overtime.

Pacheco rebounded from the fumble to rush for 86 yards on 15 carries, and Smith-Schuster and tight end Travis Kelce finished with 10 catches apiece. Smith-Schuster had 88 and Kelce had 105 of Mahomes' 336 yards on the day.

Somehow, the Chiefs accumulated more than 500 yards of offense while nearly losing to the league's worst team. They narrowly clinched a seventh straight division title, tying the Los Angeles Rams for the second-longest streak of consecutive division titles since the AFL-NFL merger in 1970, only behind the New England Patriots of the 2010s.

"When you start every single season, the first thing we get told when we first walk in is let's win the AFC West," said Mahomes, who has never participated in a season that didn't end with a division crown. "We accomplished our first goal, so, our next goal is to try to establish home-field advantage."

At the time, the Chiefs needed help. Someone had to beat the Buffalo Bills, who owned the head-to-head tiebreaker with the Chiefs.

"It's not in our hands," added the quarterback. "We can do our best to be ready in case we get that opportunity, and then win the Super Bowl." ∎

Playing in his home state of Texas for the first time in his NFL career, Patrick Mahomes completed 36 passes for 336 yards and two touchdowns.

Chiefs 24, Seahawks 10
December 24, 2022 • Kansas City, Missouri

DEFENSE WINS CHRISTMAS

Chiefs Limit Seahawks, Finally Play Clean Game in Comfortable Win

With the AFC West wrapped up once again, the Kansas City Chiefs turned their attention to closing the rest of the 2022 season strong, beginning with a Christmas Eve, Saturday game against the Seattle Seahawks in a cold environment at GEHA Field at Arrowhead Stadium.

This holiday season, Kansas City's wish list included a Buffalo loss at some point during the final three weeks of the season. If they could take care of the Seahawks — and then the Denver Broncos in Week 17 and Las Vegas Raiders in Week 18 — a Bills loss would grant them a bye in the AFC and home-field advantage throughout the postseason.

In the meantime, all they could control were their efforts in defeating the Seahawks. One might think that would be an easy task given the teams' records, but Kansas City was coming off back-to-back scares against the lowly Denver Broncos and Houston Texans.

As of late, it seemed as though a loss might be waiting to happen — it was Week 16, and the Chiefs hadn't played a turnover-free game since Week 5. Six of the nine games in that span included multiple turnovers.

Kansas City opened the scoring with a first-quarter pop pass to wide receiver Kadarius Toney, who ran his only catch of the game in for an 8-yard touchdown. In the second quarter, running back Jerick McKinnon made it 14-0 with an 8-yard touchdown catch out of the flat.

A 32-yard reception by running back Isiah Pacheco set up Chiefs kicker Harrison Butker for a 47-yard field goal, and Kansas City went into halftime up 17-3. After a week of chatter regarding the kicking game, Butker also made all of his extra points.

The Chiefs' defense swarmed the Seahawks on a day in which the offense didn't see much consistency. Seattle left the offense on the field for fourth down on six occasions during the game, and Kansas City stopped it three times.

"The defense was playing well and so we didn't force anything on the offensive side, although we were trying to score touchdowns," said head coach Andy Reid. "You don't want to slight that, we just — things weren't clicking. But, if it weren't for the defense playing so well, then that could've been a real issue."

Kansas City linebacker Nick Bolton was good in open space, leading the team with a jaw-dropping 17 tackles. Defensive tackle Chris Jones and rookie defensive end George Karlaftis each sacked Seattle quarterback Geno Smith, who finished 25-of-40 for 215

Travis Kelce's relaxed and comfortable fit matched Kansas City's performance in an easy win over Seattle.

yards, a touchdown, and a fourth-quarter interception, made by safety Juan Thornhill in the end zone.

"We knew we were capable of it," said safety Justin Reid of the defense. "It's just about going out there and doing it, though — not just saying it, going out there and executing it. Really putting it all together and this is the time of year to piece it all together. This is when you want your good teams to start getting hot and get ready to make that big run in January."

Cornerback L'Jarius Sneed and the Chiefs allowed 81 yards to wide receiver DK Metcalf, but he only made one catch over 11 yards all afternoon.

"That was the scheme that [defensive coordinator Steve Spagnuolo] had set up going in," said Reid. "I thought he did a nice job, that's a good football player right there. And so, Sneed is a good football player too, so matching them up, I thought, that was a smart thing by Spags. I thought our coaches did have a good game plan together too. My hat goes off to them."

Following Thornhill's pick, Chiefs quarterback Patrick Mahomes sought out Travis Kelce, who caught 20 and 52-yard passes on back-to-back plays. The two chunk receptions helped give Kelce 113 yards on the day.

Knocking at the goal line, Mahomes scrambled from 3 yards out, using one hand to propel his diving arm to touch the pylon, putting Kansas City up 24-3.

A late touchdown by Seattle would make it a 24-10 final, but the Chiefs wouldn't mind — they earned the win, completing the game without a turnover. ∎

The Kansas City defense matched its lowest point total allowed on the season at 10, equaling the Week 12 effort against the Rams.

SACK NATION RISES

New Defensive Line Coach Joe Cullen Provides a Jolt

To many outside the building, the Kansas City Chiefs made a subtle change in early February of 2022, when they decided to hire the 54-year-old Joe Cullen, who replaced Brandon Daly. Daly shifted to coaching Kansas City's linebackers.

It could easily be argued at the time that change was necessary. Though the Chiefs were among the top five in the league in pressure rate in 2021, the team had trouble finishing, coming in the bottom five in the league with only 31 sacks.

Kansas City's best sack number came from defensive lineman Chris Jones, with 9.0. A beginning-of-the-season experiment to move Jones to a primary defensive end had failed, and the next best player on the team when it came to sacks was Frank Clark, with only 4.5.

After the Tennessee Titans sacked Cincinnati Bengals quarterback Joe Burrow *nine* times in their Divisional Round loss, the Chiefs managed to get to Burrow only one time in their losing effort in the 2021 AFC Championship game.

That sack came from defensive end Melvin Ingram, who opted to play elsewhere in 2022.

The Chiefs knew, at the very least, Cullen would bring in a long track record of expertise. He had been an NFL defensive line coach in 15 different seasons for five different teams: the Detroit Lions (2006-2008), the Jaguars (2010-2012), the Cleveland Browns (2013), the Tampa Bay Buccaneers (2014-2015), and the Baltimore Ravens (2016-2020).

In early August, Cullen turned a lot of heads with his words after a training camp practice.

"Our first goal always here is to hoist that Lombardi Trophy," said Cullen. "And for us to get there — to get the opportunity to do that — [Jones] has to have a career year. That means not only in the stats of sacking the quarterback but knocking the run out. That's something that we've stressed — him having his best year. And not only him, but all of us in the room and myself as a coach and us as coaches. That's what we're trying to get with Chris — and he's really working towards that."

A career year? Really? Should we laugh?

Jones' best year of his career had been in 2018 — y'know — *four years ago,* when he finished with 15.5 sacks. He had not had a double-digit year since.

Returning to being a primary defensive tackle, Jones matched his career-high with 15.5 in 2022, finishing as a finalist for defensive player of the year. Asked many times throughout the year about how he had been so resurgent, Jones credited Cullen, as well as his assistant, Terry Bradden.

"I think it's an accumulation of the D-line room — unselfish guys," said Jones again in January, before continuing. "The D-line coaches, starting with Joe Cullen, assistant Terry Bradden staying with me before

Defensive tackle Chris Jones sacks Bengals quarterback Joe Burrow during the AFC championship game. Jones matched his career high with 15.5 sacks in 2018.

and after practice, me committing to be the leader — be the best — committing to improving my pass rush from last year, me committing to making sure I put the extra work in. And it shows. It shows. I give all the credit to my D-line being unselfish — some guys taking two, three people at a time, so I can get the one-on-one."

Aided by Jones' 15.5 number, the Chiefs went from bottom five to top two in team sacks in 2022, finishing the regular season with 55.0, only behind their Super Bowl LVII adversary, the Philadelphia Eagles. The Chiefs were first in the league with 178 quarterback pressures and fifth in blitz percentage.

The Chiefs had three players in the defensive line room with five or more sacks: rookie George Karlaftis (6.0), Frank Clark (5.0), and Mike Danna (5.0). Under Cullen's watch, longtime veteran Carlos Dunlap recorded the prestigious 100th sack of his career.

In last year's AFC Championship game, Burrow remained protected and comfortable. In this year's edition, featuring the same teams, Burrow was ambushed. Jones recorded sacks one and two of his career, hitting him five times. The Chiefs hit Burrow 12 times as a team, taking him down five times.

"Sack Nation," a term coined by Jones a long time ago, had returned.

Nobody was laughing at Cullen when he took the podium in January, and he was reminded of his words in the St. Joseph heat.

"Well, I think when you look at — there's been a lot of guys that have played really well and have what we call 'career years' at every level on the defense and on offense," said Cullen. "Now when you look at Chris, for us to be where we wanted to be right now in this position, we just said that he had to have his best year. We feel — and I've been with him one year — Chris has done everything. He's put the work in.

"When you put the work in, usually the results happen. He came back in great shape, he worked in the offseason, he had a great training camp and he just carried it over. He just kept chopping one day at a time, working." ■

Rookie defensive end George Karlaftis sacks Seattle Seahawks quarterback Geno Smith during a December game. Karlaftis had 6.0 sacks during the 2022 regular season.

Chiefs 27, Broncos 24
January 1, 2023 • Kansas City, Missouri

NEW COACH, SAME RESULT

Chiefs Let Broncos Hang Around Again Before Delivering Knockout Blow

The Kansas City Chiefs welcomed the Denver Broncos to GEHA Field at Arrowhead Stadium on New Year's Day for a Noon kickoff.

Many view the changing from one year to the next as the perfect time for new beginnings, and the Broncos fed into that theme perfectly as they arrived to Arrowhead with a new head coach — firing Nathaniel Hackett midway through his first season and turning the team over to an interim head coach, Jerry Rosburg, who had been serving Denver as a senior assistant.

The coaching change appeared to give the Broncos an energy boost in Week 17. Under Rosburg, Denver quarterback Russell Wilson seemed more at ease, and — just like in the game three weeks earlier at its home stadium — the Broncos hung around with the Chiefs.

Denver even held a 17-13 lead midway through the second quarter.

After three straight punts to start the half, the Chiefs answered. Quarterback Patrick Mahomes connected with tight end Blake Bell in the middle of the field, and Bell turned upfield, taking it seven more yards and running through safety Kareem Jackson for the touchdown.

Bell — in his second game back from a preseason hip injury — put the Chiefs up 20-17 early in the fourth quarter.

"Hats off and credit to the strength staff in the training room and getting me right in there," said Bell. "It was a long journey. I've been excited and each and every week I've been back, I'm trying to get better each

week and kind of knock the rust off. But like I said, I'm just happy to be out there with my boys and back in the locker room."

On the next drive, Wilson threw a ball into traffic, and Chiefs cornerback L'Jarius Sneed intercepted the football. Sneed returned the pick to the Denver 17, setting the Kansas City offense up with ideal field position.

On second-and-goal at the 3, running back Jerick McKinnon motioned to Mahomes' left before the snap, then leaked out to the left. Mahomes floated a pass to the back for McKinnon's second touchdown of the game and Mahomes' 40th on the season.

With his two receiving touchdowns in the game, McKinnon became the first running back since 1970 to have such a score in five consecutive games.

"I couldn't have done any of it without my teammates," said McKinnon. "The O-line is blocking on a whole other level right now. Pat is on a whole other level right now."

Mahomes overcame an early-game end-zone interception to finish 29-of-42 for 328 yards, three touchdowns and an interception in what became an eventual 27-24 win.

The 300-plus yards allowed for Mahomes to surpass the 5,000-yard mark on the season for the second time in his five-year career as a starter.

Stat line aside, there were periods during the game in which the quarterback looked to be missing his mark — but Mahomes kept passing. Wide receiver Kadarius

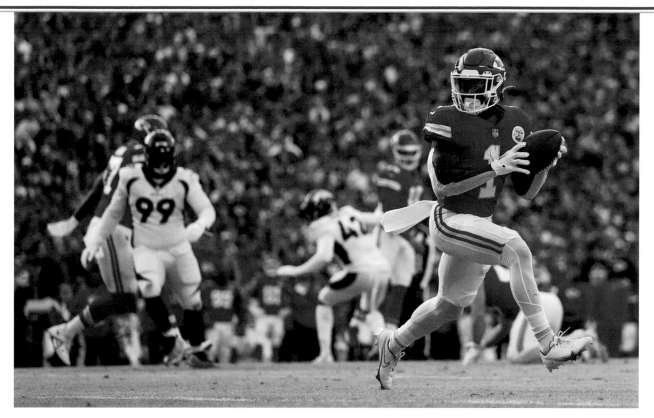

Jerick McKinnon had a nice day through the air, catching five passes for 52 yards and two touchdowns.

Toney had a career-high 71 yards, including a deep pass down the right sideline for 38 yards.

"You've all seen him when he gets the ball and he can make people miss and make stuff happen," said Mahomes. "I don't think people have really seen him run those deep routes yet."

The Chiefs stuck with Toney as its punt returner even after an early fumble.

"He doesn't have a lot of experience at doing this, but you keep that ball in the other hand – keep it on the outside," said Reid. "And so, it's great for him to learn that... We're blessed to have him. He came right back and made a huge play for us. And he's a good football player. So, we'll get that all worked out. But he just needs time, experience doing it."

Wilson gave the Broncos a 10-6 lead in the first quarter with a 16-yard touchdown run. He later threw a perfect ball to Albert Okwuegbunam for a 25-yard touchdown reception to take back the lead in the third quarter. The quarterback's second touchdown run that came late in the fourth quarter narrowed the gap to 27-24.

Wilson got the ball back with just under four minutes to go, and he would lead Denver all the way to midfield before being sacked by Kansas City defensive tackle Chris Jones on fourth down.

"Shoot, it's part of who he is now," Chiefs linebacker Willie Gay Jr. said of Jones. "We know he's going to do his part and make big plays like that. It's natural — it's second nature."

Jones' sack sealed Kansas City's 13th win on the season and set them up to root for the Cincinnati Bengals, as they hosted the Buffalo Bills the next day on *Monday Night Football*.

Nobody could have predicted what was in store for the league over the next 24 hours. ∎

Chiefs 31, Raiders 13

January 7, 2023 • Las Vegas, Nevada

DOMINATION IN THE DESERT

Complete Victory Over Raiders Propels Chiefs to Playoffs, Top Seed

As the Kansas City Chiefs traveled to play the Las Vegas Raiders on a Saturday for their final game of the 2022 season, both teams knew the world would be watching.

Five days earlier, the NFL had stopped in its tracks.

Midway through the consensus game of the year — a nationally-televised Monday Night Football matchup between the Buffalo Bills and Cincinnati Bengals — Bills safety Damar Hamlin collapsed. Medical personnel rushed the field, surrounding Hamlin before providing emergency treatment and eventually taking him away in an ambulance.

Bills head coach Sean McDermott and Bengals head coach Zac Taylor pulled their teams off the field, and the Bills flew home. Hamlin stayed overnight at the University of Cincinnati Medical Center.

As the week carried on, Hamlin's condition improved, and once it did, the league announced that the contest between the Bills and Bengals would not resume. This meant that for the Chiefs to clinch the AFC's top seed, a bye and home field advantage in the postseason, all they would need to do is beat the Raiders in Week 18.

And with that, Chiefs-Raiders, the first football following one of the scariest moments in league history, became must-watch television.

Kansas City began the game with the football and an Isiah Pacheco 5-yard run, permitting NFL fans everywhere a sigh of relief. The follow-up to the Pacheco run was a play-action make that saw wide receiver Justin Watson streaking down the left sideline.

Chiefs quarterback Patrick Mahomes hit him in stride for a 67-yard gain.

"Justin wasn't the first read, but he was kind of like an alert where you get your eyes there just to see, and he did a good job on that motion," said Chiefs quarterback Patrick Mahomes. "He didn't get the ball thrown into all practice and he was just staying alive. They played a coverage that they don't play a lot, where they played a little [Cover-2] into the field. He kind of got down that red line, the sideline, and I was able to get the ball to him and make a play."

Watson's big gain set up a short touchdown pass to running back Jerick McKinnon a few plays later. McKinnon finished with nine touchdown receptions, including at least one in six straight games to close the season. McKinnon's score began a 24-3 run for the Chiefs to start the game, with first-half touchdowns to running back Ronald Jones and wide receiver Kadarius Toney.

Officials called back Toney's first scoring attempt, erasing a touchdown play stemming from Kansas City's infamous "snow globe" huddle, in which they spun around in unison before breaking off into a play.

"It's like reindeer personnel, arctic circle, snow globe," explained Mahomes. "I just call it snow globe. It's the easiest way to say it, it's a long play call. It was something we had kind of practiced on actually last year

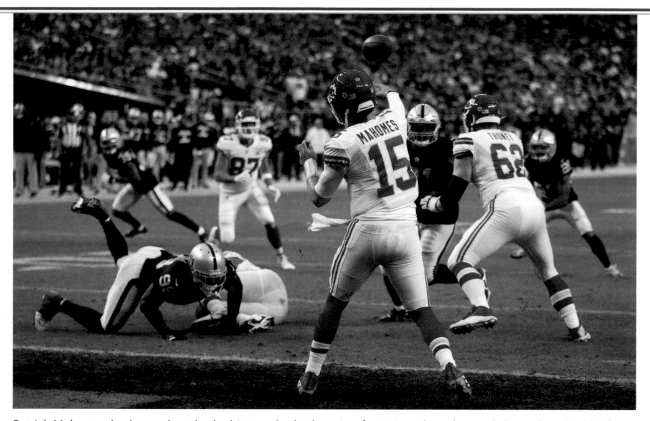

Patrick Mahomes had a modest day by his standards, throwing for 202 yards and a touchdown, but the Chiefs still cruised to a 31-13 win over the Raiders and clinched the number one seed in the AFC in the process.

of doing that, of getting confusion going and getting to the line to snap, and we didn't get the chance to run it last year... As the season went back on, I was like kind of nudging coach [Andy] Reid like, 'Hey, let's bring it back in a different way.'"

The head coach obliged.

"It's just to create a little bit of confusion, and then line up in something that's not familiar to the opposing team," added Reid. "I know the guys executed it well. We end up with a holding call, but they did good with it. And the players enjoy doing that stuff, so with a little creativity, they come up with these things. So, we just throw them out there and let them work them."

Running back Isiah Pacheco rushed for 64 yards, adding a touchdown in the fourth quarter.

In its last game before the playoffs, Kansas City played well in all three phases of the game, beating the Raiders 31-13 to clinch the conference's top seed and bye week. With the victory, the Chiefs also completed a sweep of the AFC West, and Mahomes improved to 27-3 in division games.

Quarterback Jarret Stidham, named the Las Vegas starting quarterback to close the season, had trouble getting much going against the Chiefs' star defender, Chris Jones. Jones hit Stidham six times, recording 2.5 sacks to tie his career-high at 15.5 on the season. Linebacker Nick Bolton led Kansas City with 16 tackles, and safety Juan Thornhill intercepted him.

Many questioned the Chiefs ahead of the 2022 season as they made what were considered franchise-altering roster moves. At regular-season's end — from 2021 to 2022 — the only thing that changed for them was not needing to play in the Wild Card Round. ■

THE HARD WAY

How the Chiefs Persevered and Earned the No. 1 Seed

On Monday night, January 2, in Cincinnati, the National Football League faced a dire circumstance.

With Kansas City — and the football-watching world — taking in the consensus "game of the year" between the Buffalo Bills and Cincinnati Bengals, Buffalo safety Damar Hamlin collapsed, needing immediate medical attention.

Hamlin received CPR before being transported in an ambulance to the University of Cincinnati Medical Center. The Bills weren't sure if their teammate would live. Bills head coach Sean McDermott and Bengals head coach Zac Taylor pulled their teams off the field.

The league said the game would not resume — and Kansas City Chiefs coach Andy Reid would later go on record to say the league made the right call to stop the game.

In the days following, Hamlin made miraculous strides. He was taken off a breathing tube, allowing him to speak remotely to his Bills teammates from the hospital in Cincinnati. He returned to Buffalo, and the Players Association would present Hamlin with the Alan Page Community Service Award during the week of Super Bowl LVII.

No makeup

Considering how late the game was in the season and the high playoff seeds involved, the NFL chose not to make up the game. But that came with a problem: how would the league determine the AFC's rightful No. 1 seed?

With an uneven number of games played (16) for the Bills and Bengals — who were at the time the conference's No. 2 and No. 3 seeds, respectively — there were alternate solutions floated into the universe.

One was as an option for a bye week *or* home-field advantage. Some considered the league might suddenly add an eighth seed. The league opted to change the old rule.

The old rule

The old rule stated that in the event of a no-contest, the NFL would determine all seeding solely based on winning percentage.

Sticking to the old rule would have meant the Chiefs could clinch the bye and undisputed home-field advantage with a Week 18 win over the Las Vegas Raiders. But the league said that if the Chiefs beat the Raiders (and the Bills beat the New England Patriots) in Week 18, a Chiefs-Bills AFC title game would be played at a neutral site.

Buffalo Bills safety Damar Hamlin, who collapsed and required immediate medical attention during a January 2 game against the Cincinnati Bengals, poses for a photo during the NFL Honors in Phoenix in February 2023.

As it happened, the Chiefs took care of business against the Raiders — who opted to start Jarrett Stidham for their final two games — clinching the conference's top seed. There would be no Chiefs game on Wild Card weekend.

In addition, the only possible way Kansas City could have lost its right to host a fifth straight AFC title game would have been for the Bills to win three games in a row — against the Patriots in Week 18, on Wild Card weekend and then their Divisional Round game.

As it happened, the Bills indeed beat the Patriots in Week 18, then the Miami Dolphins in the Wild Card Round. Meanwhile, the Bengals defeated the Baltimore Ravens in the Wild Card Round, leading to *a Monday Night Football* rematch in the Divisional Round.

The Chiefs defeated the Jacksonville Jaguars to open that round, meaning the winner of Bengals-Bills in Buffalo would play the Chiefs. A Bengals win would mean the fifth straight AFC Championship at GEHA Field at Arrowhead Stadium. A Bills win, and the league would see an unprecedented neutral-site AFC Championship.

In the rematch, the Bengals crushed the Bills, 27-10, setting the stage for eventual redemption for the Chiefs. ∎

Head coach Andy Reid talks with players following the Chiefs' 31-13 win over the Las Vegas Raiders in the final game of the regular season.

Chiefs 27, Jaguars 20

January 21, 2023 • Kansas City, Missouri

SOMETIMES, IT TAKES EVERYBODY

Chiefs Overcome Injury to Mahomes to Survive and Advance

The AFC West champion Kansas City Chiefs began their 2022 playoff campaign by welcoming the surprise AFC South champion Jacksonville Jaguars to GEHA Field at Arrowhead Stadium for the Divisional Round.

The Chiefs had last seen the Jaguars in Week 10, with Kansas City coming away with a 27-17 victory. The Chiefs improved to 7-2 as the Jaguars dropped to 3-7. At the time, a playoff rematch seemed highly improbable if not impossible — but that might be a good way to describe the Jaguars' season in a nutshell.

The regular season loss against the Chiefs marked a sharp turning point for Doug Pederson's bunch, which won six of its last seven games. Kansas City head coach Andy Reid watched during his team's playoff bye as his protege, Pederson, coached his way back from a 27-0 Wild Card Round deficit to stun the Los Angeles Chargers, 31-30 — thereby clinching a return trip to Arrowhead.

The first drive of the Divisional Round could not have gone much better for Patrick Mahomes.

The quarterback threw on the run, jump-passed and side armed his way into Jaguars territory. Mahomes orchestrated a 12-play, 83-yard drive, concluding with an 8-yard touchdown to tight end Travis Kelce.

The second drive of the Divisional Round could not have gone much worse for Patrick Mahomes.

After his budding counterpart, Trevor Lawrence, answered with a touchdown to wide receiver Christian Kirk, Mahomes trotted back on the field. On third-and-6 at the Kansas City 39, Mahomes, stepped up and jumped up, finding wide receiver Justin Watson for a first down.

Seemingly in a groove, Mahomes deployed a similar strategy on the next play, but it would end in disaster. When he stepped up this time, he was met by Jacksonville linebacker Arden Key and defensive tackle Corey Peters. Mahomes managed to get the ball to tight end Blake Bell as his right ankle was crushed by Key.

With his quarterback writhing in pain, Reid called his first timeout of the game. Mahomes would stay in for five more plays before the head coach sent him to the locker room for X-rays. Mahomes did not want to go.

"I wanted just to continue to play," said Mahomes. "I told them I would do it at halftime but coach, in the best interest of me, just made — he made me go back there and get that X-ray before he put me back in the game."

Harrison Butker connected on a 50-yard field goal

Defensive tackle Derrick Nnadi celebrates a sack of Jacksonville quarterback Trevor Lawrence in the 27-20 Kansas City win.

to give the Chiefs a 10-7 lead, and defensive end Frank Clark sacked Lawrence to help force a Jacksonville punt. As the athletic training staff tested Mahomes in the locker room, backup Chad Henne entered the Divisional round for the second time in three seasons.

Henne showed no sign of nervousness as Kansas City began its drive on the 2-yard line.

The veteran backup's first pass to Kelce provided some confidence — and the space necessary to work. Henne went 5-of-7 for 23 yards on the drive, finishing the 12-play, 98-yard drive with a touchdown pass to Kelce.

"Everybody trusted Chad," said Reid. "That's the best part. That's the way he handles himself — and the confidence the guys have in him... Chad did a nice job of getting the ball out on time. And the O-line did a nice job."

Running back Isiah Pacheco's 39-yard bounce-and-run to the outside — part of his 12-carry 95-yard playoff debut — alleviated some of the pressure on Henne. The Chiefs led the Jaguars 17-10 at halftime.

With Mahomes' X-rays confirmed as negative, he reentered the game in the second half. With Mahomes clearly ailing, Kansas City punted on its first two drives. Meanwhile, the defense kept getting him the ball back.

"When he goes down, we got to up our level of play and try to give the offense as many opportunities as possible down the stretch," said linebacker Nick Bolton, who led the team with 10 tackles. "I feel like on defense, we did a hell of a job winning key situations and forcing field goals when we needed to."

Mahomes began to look a little more like himself on the third drive after his return, as his 27-yard pass to tight end Noah Gray set up another 50-yard field goal, which Butker hit, making it 20-10 Chiefs entering the final quarter.

Jacksonville kept the pressure on, narrowing the gap to three points as running back Travis Etienne scored a 4-yard touchdown. With his team only up a score, Mahomes fought through the pain, stepping up high in the pocket and jumping off his left foot to get to wide receiver Marquez Valdes-Scantling for a 6-yard touchdown.

Backup quarterback Chad Henne filled in admirably for an injured Patrick Mahomes, completing 5-of-7 passes for 23 yards and a touchdown.

"I saw that I had zero coverage, just one on one with that guy," said Valdes-Scantling. "The back motioned out, the linebacker went with him. I knew they were going to double Trav, so it left me one on one. I just knew that I had to get across and let Pat find me."

The Chiefs' touchdown made it 27-17, and — keeping with the theme of everybody doing their part with Mahomes playing hurt — Butker thwarted what looked to be a dangerous return by Jamal Agnew with a diving tackle.

The Chiefs forced two turnovers in the fourth quarter — a Bolton fumble recovery and a Jaylen Watson interception — and one more Jaguars field goal proved too little, too late.

Thanks to a true team victory, Kansas City was headed to its fifth straight AFC Championship game — and the fifth straight it would host if the Cincinnati Bengals could beat the Buffalo Bills the following day. ■

Above: Chad Henne shakes hands with team president Mark Donovan after doing his part to help the Chiefs advance to the AFC Championship. Opposite: Marquez Valdes-Scantling only had one catch in the game, but it was a notable fourth quarter touchdown.

Chiefs 23, Bengals 20

January 29, 2023 • Kansas City, Missouri

'DON'T EVER DISRESPECT ARROWHEAD'

Chiefs Walk the Walk, Book a Return Trip to the Super Bowl

Thanks to the Cincinnati Bengals' dominant 27-10 win over the Buffalo Bills in the Divisional Round, the Kansas City Chiefs avoided having to travel to Atlanta, Georgia, for a neutral-site AFC Championship game.

For the fifth straight season, the title game would take place in the comfort of their home stadium. What wasn't as comfortable was the opponent up ahead: the Cincinnati Bengals, who had won their last three head-to-head matchups, including last year's AFC Championship.

And Cincinnati was hardly shy in reminding anybody who would listen. During the Bengals' Divisional Round win, cornerback Mike Hilton looked directly in an NFL Films camera so that he could tell the world how much he was looking forward to his team returning to "Burrowhead."

Hilton's fellow cornerback, Eli Apple, used Twitter to taunt the Bills after their game, and Cincinnati mayor Aftab Pureval teased the Chiefs in a cringeworthy video shared to his social media accounts.

In the week leading up to the game, the Chiefs hardly engaged in the chatter. But on the Friday before it — in the final press conference of the week — defensive tackle Chris Jones sarcastically referenced "Burrowhead" three times, closing with a stone-cold message.

"Take care. See y'all at Burrowhead," Jones said, as he walked off.

Having been diagnosed with a high-ankle sprain in Kansas City's Divisional Round win over the Jacksonville Jaguars, quarterback Patrick Mahomes underwent intense treatment all week. Had it been the regular season, maybe the quarterback may have missed at least a game or two, but a trip to the Super Bowl hung in the balance.

"He gave me no opportunity to not think he wasn't going to play," said Chiefs head coach Andy Reid. "He didn't ever miss a snap. Our players, our team, coaches, we are all lucky to have him in that position. The mindset carries over to everybody. There was no denying that he was going to play."

Mahomes instilled confidence in his athletic training staff and teammates as he pushed the ball down the field to begin the game with back-to-back drives resulting in Kansas City field goals. Without three starting offensive linemen, Cincinnati struggled to protect Burrow, allowing the Chiefs' defensive front to set the tone early.

That would be a key for Kansas City, which lost

Travis Kelce, Patrick Mahomes, and the Chiefs appeared in their fifth straight AFC Championship, and clinched a spot in the Super Bowl for the second time in three years.

cornerback L'Jarius Sneed due to a concussion just four plays into the game, meaning three rookies — first-rounder Trent McDuffie, fourth-rounder Joshua Williams, and seventh-rounder Jaylen Watson — would man the defensive secondary.

Kansas City recorded sacks on the Bengals' first eight offensive plays, resulting in two empty possessions to start the game.

Finally, on their third try, the Bengals responded with a field goal of their own, cutting the Chiefs' lead to 6-3 midway through the second quarter.

Everybody knew about Mahomes' injury throughout the week, but there was less available information on tight end Travis Kelce, who reportedly injured his back on the last play of Friday practice heading into the weekend.

"Man, I was going through it, for sure," said Kelce. "I wasn't sure if I was going to be able to do it, but we have the best training staff in the entire NFL. My guy (assistant athletic trainer) David Glover... everybody in this building has been unbelievable getting me right."

A true game-time decision, Kelce passed his pregame workout, and that was fortunate for Kansas City, especially as he scored the first touchdown of the game late in the second quarter. At the Cincinnati 14 on fourth-and-1, Reid left the offense on the field, providing Mahomes with extra protection. Mahomes shifted to his right, seeing Kelce with only one man defending him in the end zone.

The quarterback flicked the ball to his tight end for the 14-yard touchdown and 13-3 lead. The Chiefs took a 13-6 lead into the halftime locker room.

Targeting wide receiver Tee Higgins against Watson in the second quarter, Burrow was intercepted. That did not stop him from trying again to start the third quarter, and this time, Higgins plucked the ball out of the air between Watson and safety Juan Thornhill for a touchdown, tying the game at 13.

In a game defined by physicality, the Chiefs lost three receivers to injury during the game. After fighting

The Kansas City defense kept quarterback Joe Burrow on the move, sacking him five times and forcing him into two interceptions.

through injury to play for the first time since Week 9, wide receiver Mecole Hardman hurt himself again. Both wide receiver JuJu Smith-Schuster and Kadarius Toney also went down.

That meant Kansas City would need wide receiver Marquez Valdes-Scantling to play an even greater role than he had all year. On third-and-10, Mahomes saw Valdes-Scantling down the field, covered by only one man.

"I was like the last read on that play and it was like a zero-coverage to me and the cornerback," recalled Valdes-Scantling. "I think they doubled Trav — he was the first read. And once I [saw] that, the safety trigger on Trav and the corner was outside leverage I was like, 'Yo, Pat, throw me the ball.' I threw my hand up."

For the second straight playoff game, Valdes-Scantling was in the end zone — and that was after he had two receiving touchdowns all season. He finished leading the Chiefs with six catches for 116 yards, exceeding the 100-yard mark for only the second time all season.

Cincinnati punted on the next drive, and Kansas City had control. But a fluke fumble by Mahomes would change that.

"[The ball] just slipped right out of my hand," said Mahomes, "and obviously I tried to pick it up and I wasn't able to do that."

The Bengals recovered, and starting in Chiefs' territory, tied the game shortly after as running back Samaje Perine ran it in from 2 yards out.

Locked in a 20-20 tie, the teams exchanged several fourth-quarter possessions before Cincinnati took over just before the two-minute warning.

Burrow quieted Arrowhead a bit after a third-and-long conversion to tight end Hayden Hurst, but the Chiefs defense sustained the pressure it was delivering all game.

In the three previous matchups between the two teams — all wins for the Bengals — Kansas City struggled to make Burrow uncomfortable, but that was not the case on this day, as the Chiefs had already recorded 4.0 sacks by this point.

With the receiver group suffering from multiple injuries, Marquez Valdes-Scantling stepped up in a big way, catching six passes for 116 yards and a touchdown.

On third-and-8 at the Bengals 35 with less than a minute to go in the game, Jones got home for his second sack of the day, and Cincinnati's punt team jogged onto the field.

Rookie Skyy Moore — with three regular-season muffed punts to his name — was the man lined up to receive. Bengals punter Drue Chrisman booted a line drive, and Moore caught it cleanly at the 20. He followed his blocks, juking to the right sideline and up the field 29 yards.

Mahomes and the Chiefs took over with 30 seconds to go at their own 47.

Running back Isiah Pacheco gained six yards, and Reid took his final timeout. On third down, with a high-ankle sprain, Mahomes scrambled to his right and up the sideline. Cincinnati defensive end Joseph Ossai chased the quarterback.

Mahomes stepped out at the Bengals 42, but Ossai pushed him to the ground. The yellow flag flew.

Unnecessary roughness — and Butker, after the most challenging year of his career, had the chance for a 45-yard field goal with less than 10 seconds on the clock.

It was good — and after a kickoff to drain the final seconds, the game was over. The Chiefs were going back to the Super Bowl. The Lamar Hunt Trophy was home.

"It was a tough year with a lot of ups and downs," said Butker. "I missed more kicks than I ever have this season compared to other years. But I tried to keep the faith, kept working on my technique. Didn't give up and just so thankful for that kick to go through."

Ultra-motivated by the trash talk, Jones was likely the best player on the field for either team. He hit Burrow five times and brought him down twice at game's end, earning him an NFL Network spot after the game.

"Don't ever, ever, ever — I'm going to look right into the camera when I say this — disrespect Arrowhead," he said. "I don't care how many times you beat us. Don't ever disrespect Arrowhead Stadium." ∎

Isiah Pacheco wasn't a big factor in the rushing game with only 26 yards but excelled catching the ball with five receptions for 59 yards in the AFC Championship win.

THE FAB FIVE

Youth Movement in the Secondary Proves Key to Defensive Success

What if Christmas season could be *three* days instead of one?

That hypothetical became reality for Kansas City Chiefs defensive backs coach Dave Merritt, but it wasn't in December. Merritt's Christmas occurred from April 28, 2022, to April 30, 2022.

Those dates should sound familiar.

Over that three-day period, Chiefs general manager Brett Veach used five of his 10 NFL Draft picks to select defensive backs — something that had only occurred one other time in Chiefs history, in 1971.

On night one, Veach traded up to the No. 21 overall pick in the first round to take cornerback Trent McDuffie out of Washington. On day two, in round two, Veach selected safety Bryan Cook out of Cincinnati. On day three, Veach grabbed cornerback Joshua Williams out of Fayetteville State in round four.

Veach finished the draft by using two of three seventh-round picks to get cornerback Jaylen Watson out of Washington State and cornerback/safety Nazeeh Johnson out of Marshall.

None of the defensive backs attended the University of Michigan, but that did not stop Merritt from referencing its 1991 recruiting class, one of the greatest of all time.

"I call them the 'Fab Five' — [though] most of them weren't even born then," he said during training camp.

"We drafted five guys and I said, 'You guys need to understand that this group is very special.'"

Merritt called his shot. Little did anyone know at the time how right he was.

"It's like Christmas. You're working with the guys, trying to teach them new techniques — [and] they're all sponges. So it's been wonderful."

Kansas City did not expect that McDuffie would last *anywhere* close to its original pick, but when he made it to the 20s, Veach called up the New England Patriots, sending No. 29, No. 94 in the third round and No. 121 in the fourth round to Bill Belichick.

The Chiefs immediately knew they had a day-one starter. McDuffie would do just that, starting Week 1 against the Arizona Cardinals before pulling his hamstring. He started every game from his return in Week 9 until the end of the season, totaling 682 defensive snaps. The seventh-rounder, Watson, was next with 605 defensive snaps, followed by the fourth-rounder, Williams, with 437 defensive snaps.

Behind veteran studs Justin Reid and Juan Thornhill, Cook still managed 342 defensive snaps in sub-packages, leading the "Fab Five" with 272 special-teams snaps.

Altogether, the Fab Five accounted for 22 starts, 2,066 defensive snaps and 730 special-teams snaps.

Safety Bryan Cook bats away a pass intended for Cincinnati's Tee Higgins, leading to an interception by Joshua Williams during the AFC championship game. Cook and Williams were two of the five defensive backs the Chiefs selected in the 2022 NFL Draft.

Johnson did not get in on defense, however, Kansas City ensured he would remain on the roster when they traded veteran Rashad Fenton, a member of their Super Bowl LIV team, to the Atlanta Falcons right before the trade deadline.

Defensive coordinator Steve Spagnuolo, who has been coaching in the NFL in some capacity since 1999, has been notoriously hesitant to play rookies. He leaned in during the 2022 season.

"We didn't really know what to expect," said Spagnuolo the week after the Chiefs had clinched the AFC Championship. "I mean look it — when you draft somebody in the first round, you know, there's some higher expectations there. I feel like Trent has met them in what he's done, and we know he was out for a long stretch too. I always think that's very impressive — when you miss that much time as a rookie and then you can get back in the swing of things and Trent has not only played the corner position, but he's played nickel.

"The other guys were a little bit unknown although what we liked about them and what Brett identified was the length and some speed and some traits and you know I think the coaches have done — Dave Merritt and (Safeties Coach) Donald [D'Alesio] have done a great job with those guys to get them ready to play and so have the players. I mean they embraced it. Bryan Cook has been tremendous in terms of — I mean he's passionate about football. That's the one thing that's stuck out right from the beginning and we need as many passionate football players on our squad as we can get."

The Fab Nine?

Though not members of the Fab Five, the Chiefs also had outstanding contributions in 2022 from second-round defensive end George Karlaftis, second-round wide receiver Skyy Moore, third-round linebacker Leo Chenal, and seventh-round running back Isiah Pacheco.

Karlaftis started 17 games, recording 6.0 sacks, including 5.5 in the Chiefs' final seven games. Moore finished the year with 22 catches for 250 yards, redeeming early punt-team woes for a key return in the AFC Championship. Chenal chipped in for 35 tackles and Pacheco became the Chiefs' starting back midseason, rushing for more than 800 yards and five touchdowns

AFC title showcase

Almost all of the rookies played a role in the Chiefs' 23-20 victory over the Cincinnati Bengals in the AFC Championship.

"We didn't go into the offseason just throwing darts," said Veach. "We knew we had tough decisions to make, but at the same time, we put together a really good plan and we trusted in our process and we trusted in our coaching staff to lead these young individuals. It was crazy tonight to look up and see 35 (Jaylen Watson) has an interception, 23 (Joshua Williams) has an interception, 6 (Bryan Cook) has a tip, 24 (Skyy Moore) has the punt return, 10 (Isiah Pacheco) — he's been big all year — and George [Karlaftis] had a sack.

"The whole crew stepped up and that's what you need to do to win these types of games. It's a long season, you have to have tremendous depth. These guys were amazing all year and they'll continue to get better." ∎

Chiefs cornerback Jaylen Watson defends a pass during a November 2022 game against the Tennessee Titans. A 2022 seventh-round pick out of Washington State, Watson totaled 605 defensive snaps in his rookie season.

THE BOWLS OF THE SUPER BOWL

Plenty of Storylines to Choose from for Epic Super Bowl LVII Match Up

The NFL is fortunate when their championship game has one more significant storyline than it otherwise would have, but when the league was dealt a Super Bowl matchup between the Kansas City Chiefs and Philadelphia Eagles, those storylines wrote themselves.

The "Andy Reid" Bowl

Chiefs head coach Andy Reid began his career as head coach of the Philadelphia Eagles, taking them to four straight NFC Championship games from 2001 to 2004 — and winning the NFC Championship in 2004. Reid and the Eagles lost Super Bowl XXXIX to the New England Patriots.

After 14 years as Eagles head coach, Reid moved onto the Chiefs in 2013, turning another franchise around entirely. Reid took many members of his Philadelphia staff — including now-general manager Brett Veach — with him to Kansas City.

"14 years — that's a long time to be some place and they were 14 great years, I loved every minute of it," said Reid of his time in Philadelphia. "[Eagles chairman and CEO] Jeffrey Lurie is a phenomenal owner and did a great job for me, my family, everything. But it got to that point... I thought it would be good, and Jeffrey felt this way, would it be good for them and would it be good for me. And I appreciated his feeling on that. And we left with a ton of respect for each other. I think he does a heck of a job.

"[Eagles Executive vice president/general manager] Howie Roseman was also a part of that — he was involved. And I'm so happy for him. I don't think he gets near enough credit for what he's been able to do for that team — and replenishing. I love Philadelphia, love the city. I've been blessed, blessed to be in three phenomenal places in the NFL.

"And I'm loving every minute in Kansas City."

The "Kelce" Bowl

If the Reid connection wasn't enough, Super Bowl LVII marked the first time two brothers — Travis of the Chiefs and Jason of the Eagles — played for a championship.

"It's a cool scenario to be in," said Travis after the Chiefs' AFC Championship win. "My mom can't lose. I'll just leave it at that. It's going to be an amazing feeling, playing against him. Obviously, I respect everybody over there in the Eagles organization. You won't see me talking too much trash because of how much respect and how much I love my brother. It's definitely going to be an emotional game."

For it to happen at the end of the 2022 season was serendipitous, considering it was the same season the

Current Philadelphia Eagles coach Nick Sirianni was a Chiefs assistant from 2009 to 2012.

duo decided to launch their "New Heights" podcast, which was named as a tribute to their hometown of Cleveland Heights. Reid drafted both players.

"They're both, at heart, very competitive and compassionate, I think is the biggest thing," he said. "They care and they care about people, and they care about their game, their trade and their podcast it looks like it's unbelievable. They've got a good mesh there and a good relationship between the two of them."

The "Starkville High" Bowl

After the Eagles and Chiefs won their conference championships, Eagles wide receiver AJ Brown took to Twitter.

"Grew up 5 minutes away from each other," wrote Brown, referring to Chiefs linebacker Willie Gay Jr. "Won a state championship in high school together. Playing for a Super Bowl. The city is beyond proud."

The city Brown referred to was Starkville, Mississippi, where he and Gay won the 2015 6A Mississippi state championship together as Yellowjackets.

"We doing it my dawg, lets put on," wrote Gay in response to Brown.

The "Sirianni" Bowl

At the beginning of his coaching career, now-Eagles head coach Nick Sirianni was an assistant in Kansas City. He worked his way from a quality control coach in 2009 to wide receivers coach in 2012, but as noted, Reid brought his own assistants to Kansas City.

"When I came here, I was told Nick Sirianni is a really special coach — really a good football coach," said Reid. "But I had David [Culley]. David was my assistant head coach and he had been with me for 14 years and so, he was coming with me. And I had to make that determination to keep Nick or not, and I knew being as good as he was and the reputation he had, I knew he was going to get something. And so, it's worked out great for him."

Sirianni went to the Chargers for five seasons before becoming the Indianapolis Colts offensive coordinator in 2018. He spent three years with the Colts before he was hired as the head coach of the Eagles. ∎

Andy Reid speaks to the media during Super Bowl LVII Opening Night in Phoenix. Reid coached the Philadelphia Eagles for 14 seasons before moving on to the Chiefs in 2013.